AMERICAN VOICES

ITALIAN AMERICANS

AMERICAN VOICES

ITALIAN AMERICANS

by **Michael Witkoski**

Rourke Corporation, Inc.
Vero Beach, Florida 32964

Cover photo: Kimberly Dawson

∞The paper used in this book conforms to the American National Standard for Permanence of Paper for
Printed Library Materials, Z39.48-1984.

Library of Congress Cataloging-in-Publication Data
Witkoski, Michael, 1951-
    Italian Americans/Michael Witkoski.
       p.   cm.—(American voices)
    Includes bibliographical references and index.
    Summary: Discusses Italians who have immigrated
to the United States, their reasons for coming, where
they have settled, and how they have contributed to
their new country.
    ISBN 0-86593-137-2
    1. Italian Americans—Juvenile literature. [1. Italian
Americans.]
I. Title. III. Series.
E184.I8W68   1991   91-15428
973′.0451—dc20   CIP
                                    AC

CONTENTS

AMERICAN VOICES

ITALIAN AMERICANS

THE ITALIANS

IN NORTH AMERICA

The Italian influence on North America has been enormous. Pizza and pasta, grand opera and street festivals, business leaders and sports heroes—these are only a few of the gifts that Italian immigrants have brought to North America. There is a special quality to Italian life, and this quality has not been erased by passage across the Atlantic Ocean. Italians are among the most distinctive immigrant groups to arrive in the Western Hemisphere, and Italians have been able to become part of American and Canadian society without losing their unique identity.

The European discovery of the New World was by an Italian explorer, Christopher Columbus, and since 1492 Italians have brought many important features to the North American continent. From their food to their arts, Italians have freely shared their culture and heritage, and they have enriched and enlivened the mixture of American and Canadian life.

EXPLORING THE NEW WORLD

Italian contributions to American and Canadian life began before either the United States or Canada was established as an independent nation. In addition to Columbus, other Italians were active in charting the New World during the age of discovery.

Giovanni Caboto, better known as John Cabot, sailed in the service of the English. He explored the coast of Canada as early as 1497, and so established England's claim to land in the New World. Large stretches of North America's eastern coastline were charted by Giovanni da Verrazzano in 1524, and the New World itself was named after the Italian explorer Amerigo Vespucci, who proved that an entire continent had been discovered. Before Vespucci, many still believed that only islands lay between Europe and the Asian coast.

Although Italian adventurers took the lead in charting paths to new lands, no Italian colonies were founded in North America. The reason was simple: During this time, Italy was still split into a number of different, small countries, which were unable to afford the costs of an expensive undertaking such as founding a colony. As a result, Italians made their

Library of Congress

Italian explorer Amerigo Vespucci lends his name to the continent: America.

earliest mark on North America as individuals. Often they sailed in the service of other nations, as John Cabot did for England or Columbus did for Spain.

Such early Italian explorers were nurtured on Italy's long seafaring tradition, which came about because of its geography. As a peninsula with easy access to a number of ports, Italy offered the opportunity to use the sea as a route for transportation. This relative convenience of ocean travel later encouraged Italians to immigrate in large numbers to North America.

However, it was not until more than a hundred years after the United States was founded that Italians arrived in North America in numbers large enough to make a profound impact on life and society. The greatest waves of immigration came from 1800 through 1929. During this time, almost four million Italians crossed the ocean to the United States. They left their homeland because of unstable political or economic situations. They came to North America mostly to find opportunity.

PAESE: THE SPIRIT OF COMMUNITY

Since most Italian immigrants came from southern Italy, they carried with them a distinct Mediterranean attitude, a way of life that emphasized the importance of family, community, and religion. These three focal points are important in many cultures, of course, but they take on special strength and meaning for Italians and their descendants.

The central role of the family became a key factor in Italian life during immigration, and it remains an important trait. To Italians, the concept of family means more than the immediate, or nuclear, family. It includes what is known as the "extended family": grandparents, aunts and uncles, cousins and other relatives. The central role of the family goes back to conditions in southern Italy, known as the *Mezzogiorno*, where the family was the most highly valued social institution.

3

Conditions were often very hard in southern Italy, and people there depended upon relatives in order to survive. Italian immigrants brought this reliance upon the family with them to North America.

They also brought their community spirit. In Italy, the village or region, known as *paese* (pah•ay'zee), was very important in the lives of the people. It was second only to the family. Persons from the same area, known as *paesani* (pay•zah'nee), helped one another through difficult times and celebrated good times together. When Italians emigrated to North America, *paesani* tended to settle in the same neighborhoods. In that way, they kept their sense of connection with the world they had left behind. Immigrants who were already established could help newly arrived immigrants.

The *paese* was closely connected with religious life as well. Each village would have its special *festa*, or feast day, to honor its particular saint. On this day there would be parades, celebrations, and feasting. This sort of celebration became characteristic of Italians in the United States and Canada and has been enthusiastically embraced by non-Italians as well. In August, for example, Boston celebrates the Feast of Saint Anthony, and the *festa* of the Madonna of Mount Carmel is held every July 16 by the residents of Italian East Harlem in New York City. Such celebrations promote and preserve the unity of the Italian neighborhoods.

LIFE IN THE CITIES

Although Italy was largely an agricultural nation and most of its people earned their livings from farming, the majority of Italians who came to North America settled in cities. Their neighborhoods often were known as "Little Italies" or were named after the particular area where the immigrants had originated: "Little Sicily," "Little Calabria," or "Little

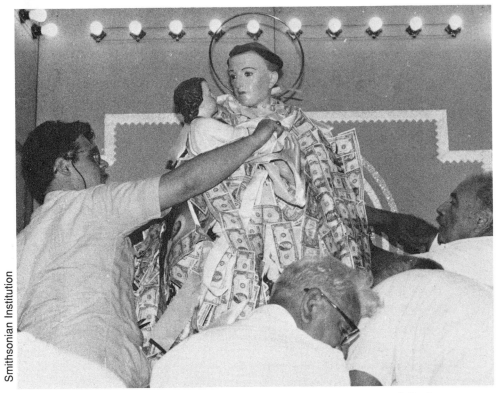

The Feast of Saint Anthony is celebrated in Boston's North End.

Napoli," for example. In these neighborhoods, Italians opened shops and restaurants, selling the traditional goods and foods of their homelands. Many of these items were adopted into North American society. From these neighborhoods Italian immigrants moved into the mainstream of American and Canadian life, achieving success in business, politics, the arts, and sports.

Rural Italians

Those Italians who did become farmers in North America generally found a much better life than the one they had left in Europe. Agriculture in Italy was difficult, especially in the south. The land in southern Italy was poor, rainfall came in the wrong season, and prices for crops were generally low.

5

When Italians arrived in the New World, they chose to specialize in farming that was quite different, and much more profitable, than the backbreaking labor they had left behind. They concentrated on fruits, vegetables, and other "truck farm" crops, which they could ship to markets in nearby towns and cities. Some of the truck farms gave rise to large food and canning companies. Other Italians settled on fertile land in California and established the wine industry in America.

OVERCOMING DIFFERENCES

The Italian experience in North America has not been without problems, however. Most Italians came to this continent during the second half of the nineteenth century and the first two decades of the twentieth century. During this period, immigrants were often feared by those already living in North America. Italians often met with prejudice, antagonism, discrimination, and sometimes even violence.

One reason for this reaction was the sheer number of Italians who came to North America in such a short period of time. Between 1870 and 1914, more than five million persons left southern Italy; this was more than one-third of the total population of that area. Many southern Italians went to South America, but a substantial portion settled in North America, especially the United States. Some of the resident Americans feared that they would be "overrun" by immigrants whose culture was, in many ways, very different from these "native" Americans' way of life.

Now that these troubled periods are part of history, and Italians have become more accepted in North American society, the true contributions of Italians to North America are being recognized.

Two Italies

Italian immigrants to the North American continent came from two sections of Italy and usually fell into one of two categories. Northern Italians were generally more prosperous, better educated, and more easily accepted into American culture. Southern Italy was a much poorer section of the country, and persons from there were frequently less well educated. In addition, their Mediterranean appearance and customs marked them more clearly as "foreigners" in North America. This set the bulk of Italian immigrants apart from others in the United States and Canada.

The language difference drove another wedge between Italian Americans and resident Anglo-Saxon Americans. Unlike immigrants from the British Isles, such as the Scots or the Irish, Italians brought to North America a language with many dialects. Until large numbers of Italians learned English, they faced this additional barrier—not only between themselves and resident Americans but also between themselves and other Italian immigrants. Other immigrant groups did not always face this obstacle.

The Bond of Religion

Religion also marked Italians as distinct. Italians are still mostly Roman Catholic in church membership, and during the period 1880 through 1914 (the peak years of Italian immigration) their religion clearly set them apart from largely Protestant North America. Even though they shared this religion with Irish, German, and Polish immigrants, Italians had a more Mediterranean approach to their methods of observing Catholicism, and that sometimes caused friction between them and their fellow Catholics.

More often, however, religion was a binding force in the lives of these immigrants. The place of religion in the lives of Italian Catholics had always been strong, and when they arrived on a new continent, they found that the Church and its institutions helped them survive and prosper. Along with mutual aid and self-help societies and associations, the Church came to hold a central place in Italian-American communities.

The blend of religious and social concern felt by Italian Catholics is probably best seen in the life of Frances Xavier Cabrini, known as "Mother Cabrini," who came to the United States in 1889 to lead the Missionary Sisters of the Sacred Heart. Mother Cabrini died in 1917 after a lifetime of devoted service to her church and people. In 1946, she was canonized a saint.

Saint Frances Xavier Cabrini, painting by Louis Jambor.

CRIME AND PREJUDICE

Not all Italians who came to North America were saints. Especially during the period of Prohibition in the United States (1920 through 1933), a number of Italians were involved in crime. The attempt to forbid the sale of alcoholic beverages during Prohibition made many Americans lawbreakers and fostered an atmosphere in which illegal activities became not only profitable but, even worse, tolerated by many average citizens.

Some Italians, like some individuals of any nationality, took advantage of this situation. Gangsters such as Al Capone, Charles "Lucky" Luciano, and Frank Nitti became legendary. This was the period when the idea of the Mafia became fixed in popular culture, and organized crime was often identified as a largely Italian operation. Movies such as *Little Caesar* (1930) showing atrocious gangland killings dramatized the dealings of such crime families as the Mafia. These crime societies had in many cases originated in Italy as brotherhoods of organized crime that later made inroads in Italian-American communities, and they are active to this day.

The image of Italian Americans suffered unfairly from these few evil people. Movies and books revealed much of both fact and fiction about this underworld, with the result that innocent Italian Americans sometimes came under suspicion. This stereotype was, of course, untrue. Others besides Italians were criminals: There were German, Irish, and Jewish members of the underworld mobs and crime syndicates. No nationality has a monopoly on either vice or virtue.

A SPECIAL VOICE

The assimilation of Italians into North American culture has been a unique one: They have retained much of their traditional culture, and much of that culture has been adopted by their non-Italian neighbors. The popular image of Italians

9

tends to focus on their public roles, their celebrations and special events. Italian cooking, especially the cuisine of southern Italy, has become widely accepted in North America and is probably the Italians' most pervasive contribution to American culture.

But that is only part of the story: Italian Americans have made their voice heard in science, the performing arts, politics, sports, music, literature, and the visual arts. They have made a lasting and positive impact on North America, and they remain a distinct and vibrant part of the social, cultural, political, and economic life of the North American continent.

THE COMMUNITY

When Italian immigrants arrived in North America, they found themselves in a new society which was often totally different from the one they had left. It was natural that the new arrivals tended to gather in communities of their own, where they could find mutual support, familiar customs, and a common heritage. Through these communities, Italian immigrants made their way into the general society.

EARLY IMMIGRANTS

Italian immigrants are found in every state of the Union and throughout all of the Canadian provinces. Before the great influx of the late 1800's, Italians who came to North America were few in number and fairly well scattered across the continent, but there were certain areas where they gathered. Even in this early period, Italians tended to remain in or near urban areas, with large numbers living in New York City, New Orleans, and San Francisco.

The reasons were simple: These early Italian immigrants were primarily artisans, craftsmen, and professionals of various sorts. Their skills and trades could be put to best use in a city. Also, because of transportation routes and other conditions in the late 1800's and early 1900's, cities in the northeastern United States attracted the majority of Italians.

New York, for example, had a concentration of Italians because it was the primary port of entry into the United States. New Orleans was congenial to Italians because of its

Latin flavor and large population of Roman Catholics. San Francisco had several attractions for Italians: They could practice their trades in the city, become commercial fishermen in the waters around San Francisco Bay, or grow crops in the rich farmland nearby.

As farmers, California's Italians tended to specialize. Either they started vineyards to produce wines or they concentrated on crops such as fruits and vegetables, which were either canned or sold in the open-air markets of San Francisco. Italians became very successful in this type of agriculture, called truck farming.

The situation in Canada was similar to that in the United States. A relatively small number of Italians, most of them from the northern section of their country, arrived prior to the 1880's. They settled throughout the nation but were concentrated in the cities of Toronto, Quebec, and Montreal.

LATER IMMIGRANTS

When the great wave of Italian immigration started in the 1870's, this situation changed dramatically. This second group of Italians came almost exclusively from the south of Italy, the *Mezzogiorno*. Instead of the diverse talents that earlier Italians had brought, this group was primarily composed of peasant farmers called *contadini*, who often lacked any specific skills or talents, especially those required by the growing industrial society of North America.

These Italians remained in the cities, especially the cities of the northeastern and the midwestern United States. New York became the urban center, having the largest number of Italians: In the years before World War I, it had more Italian residents than Florence, Venice, and Genoa combined. More Italians lived in New York City than in Rome, Italy.

Turn-of-the-century Italian emigrants take the ferry to Ellis Island in hopes of becoming citizens.

WHY THE CITY?

There were several reasons that these locations were attractive for the newly arrived immigrants.

First, the cities offered jobs. These jobs were often low-paying manual labor or work in factories, but they almost always provided more income than the immigrants had ever earned in Italy, and most of the immigrants viewed these jobs as the first step up the ladder of opportunity. In some cities, Italian immigrants came to dominate particular businesses or professions. One notable example is commercial fishing, in which Italians had the background and experience to excel. Italians virtually monopolized the fishing industry in the seacoast towns of Boston, Tampa, New Orleans, Galveston, Monterey, San Francisco, and Astoria, Oregon. In the northeastern United States, Italians were prominent in construction and the garment trade.

Second, the cities had housing for the immigrants. Many of the newly arrived Italians started life in North America living in bad conditions, even slums, but they viewed their hardships as temporary. They were determined to move on to a better life, and most of them did.

Third, Italians who arrived in cities such as New York, Chicago, or San Francisco found communities of other Italians already living there. These communities were able to help the new immigrants adapt to their new country. Earlier immigrants had formed mutual self-help societies. People from the same village or section of Italy (*paese*) tended to congregate, and these *paesani*, as they called themselves, provided fellowship and financial assistance to one another.

MUTUAL AID SOCIETIES

The Society of the Immaculate Conception of Mary, for example, was formed in Louisiana in 1904 by Sicilian immigrants. Its members paid dues. The money was used to provide health, life, and unemployment insurance, and also to help with the medical expenses of sick members. If a member died, the Society provided money for his widow.

The organization also celebrated a number of social and religious events. Regular meetings were attended during the year, and each December 8, the Feast Day of the Blessed Virgin, members of the Society held a formal procession to church, where a special Mass was celebrated. Following the service there was a dance, which raised money for charity.

Similar mutual aid societies were established in Canada. The Order of Italy, a broad-based group with political and cultural goals as well as charitable aims, was founded in 1913. In 1971, the Italian Canadian Benevolent Corporation was established, and soon it was engaged in large-scale projects, such as building a senior citizens center.

FAMILY

The traditional center of Italian life is the family. Especially

Club Fugazi in San Francisco, California, is still thriving as a social and cultural center for Americans of Italian descent.

in southern Italy, the family was essential for survival; it became the most important social institution in a country that was plagued by weak or indifferent government, poverty, and crime. The extended family, including not only the father, mother, and children but all their relatives as well, took on prime importance.

The typical Italian family had a definite structure, and great respect was given to older family members. Following in ancient Roman tradition, the father was the ruler of the family, while the mother was the emotional center. Children were expected to be dutiful and obedient, and great emphasis was placed on protecting the purity and chastity of the daughters.

The Italian immigrant experience in North America tended to strengthen the role of the family. Strangers in a land that was so different socially, religiously, and culturally, Italians sought comfort and reassurance in the institution they relied upon most: the family. Over time, it became common for observers to note the key place of the family in Italian life.

As time passed, however, and Italian Americans and Italian Canadians became more assimilated into North American society as a whole, changes took place. As is true among many well-established immigrant groups, later generations came to see themselves more as Americans than as Italians, and many moved away from the Italian-American neighborhoods to intermarry and settle wherever work, school, or other activities would take them. In the twentieth century, cars and airplanes have speeded this movement away from the family and the old neighborhoods.

Some of these changes have had the effect of weakening the traditional view of the family and the roles of its members. For Italian Americans, however, the family—the product of thousands of years of culture and history—remains an integral part of Italian life.

FESTI: CELEBRATIONS OF FAITH

Religion and the Catholic church also continue to play a large role in Italian life. Within the individual family, a series of events act as milestones. A child's first Communion, for example, and the ceremony of Confirmation, which brings a person formally into the Catholic church, are major steps toward adulthood. Weddings and funerals are momentous occasions, often marked by large and well-attended family gatherings.

In the community at large, religious festivals are a

characteristic feature of Italian life. Such events, known as a *festi*, have become familiar in almost every large American and Canadian city. The *festa* of San Gennaro in New York is one example. Another typical *festa* is that of Our Lady of Mount Carmel, held each year since 1894 in Melrose Park, a suburb of Chicago. The highlight of this *festa* is a procession of the many religious societies and organizations of the Italian community. Members of the societies carry small shrines (called *cente tabernacoli* in Italian) to honor the Virgin Mary. These shrines are elaborately decorated.

Those marching in the procession hold lighted candles. Bands play familiar hymns and sacred compositions. The focus of the parade is a life-size statue of the Virgin Mary and the Infant Jesus. As this statue is carried through the street, people step forward from the crowd to place money about the statue's base as thanks for prayers that have been granted. Vendors various foods, and others have souvenirs for sale. Carnival rides and other amusements line the side streets, and at night there are elaborate fireworks.

RETAINING THEIR ROOTS

Italian Americans created their own neighborhoods within American and Canadian cities. These neighborhoods developed a distinctly Italian ethnic atmosphere, and the culture of Italy found its way into North America through these communities. The typical foods of southern Italy, which are now so popular in fast-food restaurants and supermarkets, were first prepared and sold in these neighborhoods. As non-immigrants became exposed to the Italians, they learned more about the habits and beliefs of their new compatriots, especially the important role of the family in Italian life, the lively Italian social festivals, and the immigrants' particular brand of Catholicism. Despite many changes over time, the modern Italian-American community has managed to keep many of its distinct traits.

17

ITALY

The peninsula of Italy, which is part of the continent of Europe, stretches from the Alps in the north to the Mediterranean Sea in the south, and is well known for its boot-like shape. Italy has approximately 116,300 square miles of land, not including the two large islands of Sicily and Sardinia, totaling about 97,000 square miles and located off the peninsula's west coast.

THE LAND

Three-fourths of Italy's land is occupied by mountains or steep hills. Although good farming land is now limited, until the mid-twentieth century most Italians earned their living by agriculture. Since World War II, Italy has also become one of the leading industrial nations of Europe.

Italy is divided into three major regions: northern, central, and southern (the southern region includes Sicily and Sardinia). Each region has a distinct geography which has influenced its history and culture.

THE NORTH

In the north, a famous mountain range, the Alps, forms Italy's border with France, Switzerland, and Austria and provides protection for the extensive northern plains. This is where Italy's best farmland is found, especially in the valley of the Po River, which cuts through the plains from France in the west to the Adriatic Sea in the east. The north is also the area where most Italian industry is located.

Northern Italy is ideally suited for industry. The fertile farmland grows abundant food for the population, while the swift mountain streams provide the source of inexpensive hydroelectric power. Markets for goods are found in nearby France, Germany, and central and eastern Europe.

Important cities in northern Italy include Turin, Genoa, Milan, Bologna, Venice, and Trieste. Turin is located in the area of Italy known as the Piedmont and is headquarters for the internationally known Fiat automobile company. Genoa, located on the northwest coast, is Italy's major port and was the birthplace of Christopher Columbus.

Milan, the capital city of the area known as Lombardy, is a major financial and industrial city, as well as a fashion and design center. Bologna is mainly noted as a market hub for the region's rich agricultural produce, a role the city has filled since ancient Roman times. Venice, on the Adriatic Sea, was a major commercial and political power during the Middle Ages and the Renaissance. Now it is mainly famous for its canals and art treasures, drawing most of its wealth from tourism. Trieste, at the head of the Adriatic Sea, is a busy port and is also active in shipbuilding and the production of oil and steel.

Northern Italy has always been the wealthiest section of the nation, and its people have traditionally had the highest standard of living. Persons who immigrated to North America from this section of Italy were generally well educated and brought skills and resources with them to their new home.

CENTRAL ITALY

The geography of central and southern Italy is largely determined by the Apennines, the north-south chain of mountains which forms the "backbone" of the Italian peninsula. In many places the Apennines are quite tall, and they often break the landscape into narrow valleys where farmland is scarce. Rivers are dry and narrow in the summer months, but they can flood easily in the winter—with disastrous results. On the coasts of central Italy, there are only a few good harbors.

Major cities in central Italy include Florence, Pisa, and Rome. These places played major roles in the history of Italy and Western civilization. This part of Italy is not as industrial as the north, and the people depend upon small farms, light industry, and the services connected with government and tourism.

Today, Rome, Italy's capital city, is the seat of Italian government and the major communications center for the nation. It is also the site of Vatican City, a tiny, independent nation that is home of the Pope and the headquarters of the Roman Catholic church. With its splendid buildings, churches, and art collections, Rome is a major tourist attraction for travelers from all over the world.

Florence was one of the most important cities of the Italian Renaissance and is also a place that tourists frequently visit to see its famous paintings, sculptures, and buildings. Near the west coast is Pisa, noted for its famous leaning tower. The astronomer and physicist Galileo was born in Pisa, and he used the leaning tower to perform one of his most important experiments.

THE SOUTH

Southern Italy, which begins just south of Rome, is the poorest section of the country. The land is very bad for farming, for a number of reasons. The trees of the mountains and hills were long ago cut down and not replaced, resulting in severe erosion, which has taken away the fertile topsoil. Rainfall comes largely during the winter, rather than in the spring or summer, and this hinders the growth of crops. Until recently, when they were drained, many of the lowlands were swamps or marshes, better suited for disease than agriculture.

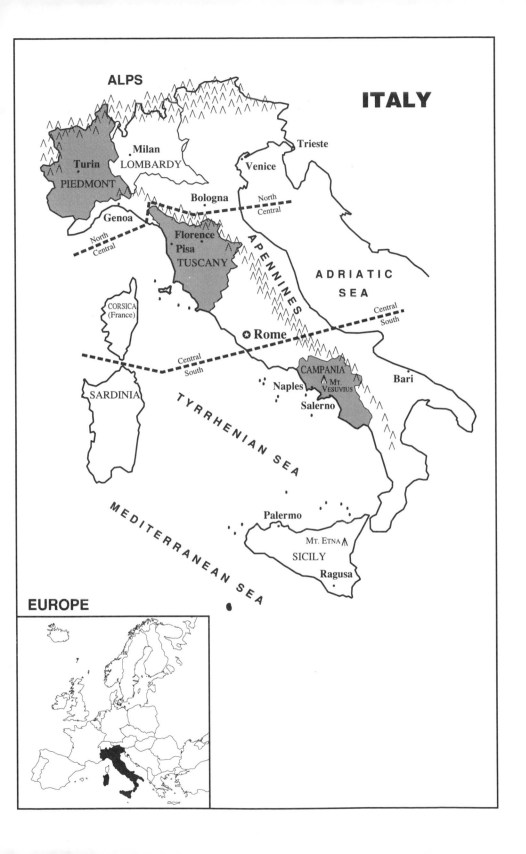

The problems of southern Italy have long been recognized. Known in Italian as the *Mezzogiorno*, the south has always had the most poverty, the highest rates of disease and death, and the most backward social conditions. For these reasons, immigrants from Italy have come largely from the south. Most of the people who came to North America from Italy came from the *Mezzogiorno*. On the peninsula, the major cities in this region are Naples, Salerno, and Bari, all seaports. On the island of Sicily, Palermo, also a port, is the capital and major metropolis.

In addition to being a port, Naples is a major communications center and has a variety of industries. It has a fairly large area of good farmland, because volcanoes in the region erupted minerals that produced rich soil. The most famous of these volcanoes is Mount Vesuvius. In A.D. 79, Mount Vesuvius erupted suddenly and violently, burying the ancient Roman cities of Pompeii and Herculaneum. This volcano is still active today.

Salerno, south of Naples in the region called Campania, is similar to its neighboring city, but on a smaller scale. On the Adriatic coast, Bari has steel, chemical, and oil plants. Palermo fits into this pattern: a seaport with a small but fertile agricultural area and diversified industry. Mount Etna, on the eastern coast of Sicily, is another famous and still-active volcano.

THE PEOPLE

The geographical division of Italy is reflected in the social, cultural, and even linguistic differences among the country's people.

PHYSICAL FEATURES

In northern and central Italy, the population is a mixture of different racial backgrounds. Residents of these sections tend

22

to be taller and have fairer complexions than Italians in the south. A number of northern Italians have blond or blondish hair, especially those who live in the Alpine regions. Because of higher economic standards, education has traditionally been better in northern Italy than in the rest of the country.

Southern Italians generally have what is called a "Mediterranean" physical appearance: olive complexion, dark hair and eyes, and a broad, short body. Because of the poverty in the south, education has usually been poor, and the illiteracy rate remained very high well into the twentieth century. At the beginning of the twentieth century, as many as 75 percent of the people in this section of the country could not read or write.

Rich and Poor

Social divisions between rich and poor, between the powerful elite and the common people, exist throughout Italy but are strongest in the *Mezzogiorno*. The importance of family and family connections, strong throughout Italy, is strongest in the south. In the past, these strong family feelings could lead to *vendettas*, deadly feuds between warring clans. As the residents of the area have become less isolated and more educated, the feuds have decreased, but the family remains a strong part of their lives.

Food and Diet

Food also reflects the division of the country. In the north, the diet includes a considerable amount of meat, chicken, and dairy products. Pasta—noodles such as macaroni and spaghetti—has only recently become a familiar sight on tables in the north. In general, the higher economic standards in this region have given a greater variety to the menu.

By contrast, southern Italy has lacked this variety. There, pasta and bread, cheap and filling, form a major portion of the meals. Meat, fish, and dairy products are less common than in the north. Lentils, a bean-like legume high in protein, are found in many meals, especially among the poorer people. Olive oil is used in cooking; in the north, butter is preferred. Because southern Italy has a warm climate, fresh vegetables and fruits form a large portion of the diet, when there is land available to grow them.

LANGUAGE

Italy's geographic divisions are reflected in its spoken language. Italian is a Romance language—that is, a descendant of the Latin that was once spoken throughout the Roman Empire. Modern Italian is a development of the version spoken in Tuscany (in central Italy) during the Middle Ages. The Tuscan dialect became the standard because of the great economic and intellectual importance of the Tuscan city of Florence during that period.

Although Tuscan became the standard language, regional variations, or dialects, flourished. Until the spread of modern communications such as radio and television, these dialects could be quite distinct. In some cases, a northern and southern Italian might not understand each other if they spoke their own dialects. Some scholars even believe that the people of Sardinia speak a separate language from Italian.

SOME COMMON CHARACTERISTICS

While there are many differences in Italian culture and life, there are also elements which unite the people. One of these is religion, since almost all Italians belong to the Catholic church. In fact, Roman Catholicism was officially the state religion of Italy until 1985.

Another common element is that most Italians live in or near cities or towns, even though most of the people were farmers until recently. During World War II, half the population worked on farms. In modern Italy, only one-sixth of the people work in agriculture. Southern Italians follow a variety of trades and professions, while northern Italians account for most of the industry and technology. The area around Milan, Turin, and Genoa in the north has the most development and greatest population density.

An appreciation of culture in its various forms is another quality shared by Italians. Italians love motion pictures, sports, and music. Holidays and festivals are celebrated with great pageantry and often include parades and processions.

THE HISTORY

Anyone who visits Italy sees and feels its history. Italy was settled by a variety of peoples—including Greeks in the south and the mysterious Etruscans in central Italy—and the peninsula was the birthplace of the world's greatest state, the Roman Empire. The Renaissance, the most important cultural movement of Western civilization, began in Italy in the 1400's (some say even earlier) and spread throughout Europe. The churches, theaters, roads, waterworks, and monuments of these long-ago people can still be visited.

A CRADLE OF WESTERN CIVILIZATION

Starting as a small village on the Tiber River, Rome became the center of an empire that stretched from the British Isles and Germany in the north to the Euphrates River and Arabia in the south. For more than a century, the Pax Romana, or "Roman Peace," brought order and stability to most of the known world.

After twelve hundred years of expansion and rule, the Roman Empire dissolved for a number of reasons. Following a long period of unrest and confusion, the city-states of northern Italy established themselves as centers of political power and intellectual achievement. During the Renaissance, cities such as Milan, Florence, Pisa, Venice, and Urbino produced artists, writers, and philosophers who made great contributions to Western civilization.

MOVING TOWARD NATIONHOOD

Italy, however, remained a land of small states. During a time when other countries, such as France and England, were uniting, Italy was divided. It was not until the French Revolution in 1789 that serious efforts to unify the country began to be made. This movement became known as the *Risorgimento*, or "resurrection." During the 1800's, popular support for a unified Italy increased, and political activists such as Giuseppe Garibaldi and Count Cavour became national heroes. The Kingdom of Italy was declared in 1861, and the entire peninsula was united in 1870.

Unification did not solve Italy's problems. Once united, Italy attempted to become a great power and compete with its powerful neighbors, but it was handicapped because of its poor economy and weak military. The *Mezzogiorno* was still impoverished, and the government largely ignored the region. One result of this neglect was the exodus of people from southern Italy that took place after 1870. Many of those Italians went to North America in search of a better life.

BECOMING A MODERN NATION

Although it fought on the winning side during World War I, Italy felt that had not received its share of the victory. In particular, Italians were disappointed in not receiving additional territory in the north and along the Adriatic coast from the defeated Austro-Hungarian Empire. Italy had also hoped to be granted some of Germany's colonies, and believed that its interests had been ignored by the other Allied powers. In 1922, after a period of unrest and violence, a dictator named Benito Mussolini and his Fascist Party took control of

Italy. Mussolini became an ally of Adolf Hitler and his Nazi Germany, and led Italy into World War II. The war was very unpopular with the Italian people, who overthrew the Fascists in 1943 and joined the Allies, including the United States, Great Britain, France.

After World War II, Italy rebuilt its economy using assistance from the United States Marshall Plan. In 1958, the country joined the European Common Market and began to update its factories and industries. In modern Europe, Italy is now recognized as a major economic power. Although many severe social problems remain, modern Italy has become much more of a progressive, egalitarian society.

WHY AMERICA?

The flow of Italians to the North American continent has taken place over a span of five hundred years. During that time, the millions of Italians who have left their homeland have had different reasons for making such a bold journey.

Some came seeking adventure. Others had been fairly well-off in Italy but believed they could do even better in the New World. A fairly large number came because of political unrest, especially after Italy was unified. Following unification in 1870, the vast majority of Italians who immigrated to North America left their homes because of extremely bad economic conditions. They were searching for opportunities in the United States and Canada which they could not find in Italy.

EXPLORERS AND ADVENTURERS

The first Italians who sailed to North America were explorers and adventurers. They were caught up in the excitement that swept Europe after the discovery of the new lands to the west. Italians helped chart the unknown territories, and they were active in expeditions of the English, French, and Spanish. At this time, Italy itself was divided into many small states that could not afford to support expeditions or establish their own colonies.

Typical of such Italian adventurers was Henri de Tonty. He came to North America in 1678 and was second in command to the great French explorer Robert Cavalier, Sieur de La Salle. Tonty built the first sailing ship seen on the Great

28

Lakes. He explored the Mississippi River with La Salle, and in 1686 he established the first European settlement in what is now the state of Arkansas.

ARTISANS AND POLITICAL LEADERS

Individual Italians lived and worked in the new colonies set up in North America. Italian glass makers were among the first settlers in the English colony at Jamestown, Virginia. Italian silk workers brought their craft to Georgia and Pennsylvania. In the west, an Italian Catholic priest, the Reverend Eusebio Francisco Kino, founded twenty-four missions in a territory that is present-day Arizona and northern Mexico. Father Kino introduced new kinds of crops and taught the Native Americans new ways to raise livestock.

These early Italian immigrants were generally well educated, skilled in some profession or art, and usually from prosperous and advanced northern Italy. Those who came from this area included painters, sculptors, musicians, artisans, and writers.

An excellent example of these early immigrants is Philip Mazzei, who was born in 1730 near Florence. Educated as a doctor, he met Benjamin Franklin in London and began a correspondence with Thomas Jefferson. Mazzei came to Virginia in 1773 to farm and met Jefferson. They became friends and discovered that they shared many ideas about government and politics. Mazzei may have influenced the ideas behind the Declaration of Independence. Mazzei was elected to public office in Virginia and helped to revise the legal code of his adopted state. During the American Revolution, he went back to Europe to raise money for the colonists in their struggle against Great Britain. He later published a four-volume history of the new nation.

In the period after the American Revolution and before the Civil War, the flow of Italians to the United States and Canada increased but remained relatively small. Some came seeking

Philip Mazzei

better personal opportunity, others began to make the voyage for political reasons. Again, part of the reason for this low number of immigrants was that Italy was not yet a nation, but a collection of small states bound by a similar language. Italians emigrated as individuals, not as Italians.

Although most Italians tended to settle in large cities, by the middle of the nineteenth century they were found throughout Canada and in every state of the Union. Some of the Italian immigrants were quite colorful characters. One of the most interesting was named Decimus et Ultimus Barziza. His name means "Tenth and Last," because he was the tenth and final child in the Barziza family. Like many other Italian Americans, Barziza fought in the Civil War. He was an officer in the Confederate army and participated in many battles, including the Battle of Gettysburg. Captured by Union troops, Barziza escaped from the train that was taking him to prison.

After the war, he became a lawyer in Texas and a prominent member of the state legislature.

SEEKING POLITICAL UNION

Italians did not leave Italy for North America in large numbers until the middle of the nineteenth century, when a series of political upheavals and wars occurred in Europe. Such wars were not new to Europe: Kings, princes, and religious leaders had vied for power during the many centuries since the Roman Empire's collapse. The revolutions that took place toward the middle of the ninetcenth century were all part of a larger transition, as small city-states consolidated to become the large nations of modern Europe.

The idea of making one nation out of the smaller city-states of the Italian peninsula was not new. After the French Revolution of 1789, a feeling of nationalism had begun to grow among the people of the Italian peninsula. People were disgusted with their existing governments and longed for the grand old days of the Roman Republic. Nothing much came of this dream, however: The movement toward unity was resisted by the various European governments, because it would change the existing situation. They were not ready to deal with another nation in their midst. Then came other wars throughout Europe in the mid-1800's.

The political maneuverings that would eventually lead to modern Italy were in the works even as these revolutions were taking place. Camillo di Cavour, the prime minister of Sardinia, was a shrewd politician who managed to manipulate other European powers to take advantage of both them and the Italian patriots. He eventually convinced France to fight Austria, which held power over large parts of northern Italy. Although France eventually made a separate peace with Austria, Cavour was able to get part of Austria's former holdings for Sardinia and its king, and he later used the popular revolutionaries—including their fiery leader in the south, Giuseppe Garibaldi—to gather other parts of Italy under his domain. Eventually, in 1861, all of Italy except Rome and Venetia became the Kingdom of Italy, and by 1870 Rome and Venetia had joined, too.

During the stormy times leading up to this unification, many Italian patriots were put in prison or otherwise harassed, and many fled the country because they were being persecuted for their political beliefs and activities. Garibaldi, the great military and nationalist revolutionary himself, lived in New York in 1850 and 1851. He launched a campaign that helped gain his nation's unification. It is no surprise, therefore, that Italian immigration to the United States shot up from less than two thousand, between 1841 and 1850, to more than nine thousand, between 1851 and 1860, the year before the Kingdom of Italy was formed.

UNIFICATION: MORE HARD TIMES FOR ITALIANS

Conditions in Italy became worse after the nation was fully unified in the 1870. Many in Italy, especially in the south, had hoped that a country of their own would solve many of their problems. Unfortunately, this was not the case: Conditions in southern Italy became worse after unification. The new government was dominated by men from northern Italy who put available resources into their own section of the country, leaving the south without the help it needed.

Southern Italy was already poor. Most of the people who lived there depended upon agriculture, but much of the soil was unfavorable for farming. The region lacked industry and had little chance for economic growth. Its population was too large for its resources, and many of its people were uneducated, even illiterate. Worse, southern Italy was a closed society, controlled by a few wealthy landowners, the Catholic church, and the government.

There was little opportunity for people in southern Italy. Many believed that there was only one hope: to leave for a new land. From the 1870's on, most southern Italians believed this opportunity would be found in North America.

DECIDING TO LEAVE THE HOMELAND

There were several reasons for this belief. First, Italians had heard that America and Canada offered what Italy denied them. They could find good soil for farming, high pay for their work, low taxes on their earnings, no compulsory military service, and greater personal freedom.

Second, Italians who had already made the move sent back money to their relatives and urged them to come to America and Canada. People in Italy knew that they would have support and assistance of earlier Italian emigrants when they arrived in the new country.

Third, many Italians were recruited by *padroni*, work bosses or agents who brought laborers over to North America to work on farms or in factories. These middlemen had become common during the age when Canada and the United States were closing the frontier and becoming industrialized nations. North America welcomed both skilled and unskilled labor from abroad.

A fourth reason, and most important in a practical sense, was the development of the steamship. This advance in transportation made ocean passage possible for large numbers of persons.

THE IMMIGRANT FLOOD

While some Italians still left home for political reasons, most now departed because of hard economic times. Many of these Italians went to South America during the harvest season and then returned to Italy when their work was done. Those who came to North America, however, tended to remain and

33

Many immigrant families became farm workers and manual laborers; even the children worked to earn more money.

make the continent their new home. They sent back money to their families in Italy, and encouraged other Italians to immigrate.

Starting in the 1870's, and growing rapidly after 1880, most Italian immigration came from the south. So large was the movement that, between 1870 and 1914, more than one-third of the population of southern Italy immigrated, and most of them went to the United States or Canada.

The high-water mark of Italian immigration to North America came between 1880 and 1920. This was a period when conditions in Italy were especially bad, particularly in the south. Overpopulated, with poor land for farming, a high tax rate, and widespread lack of education, southern Italy was an area which offered little hope to the people who lived there. These conditions grew worse because of bad weather during the last part of the 1890's and the turmoil in the Italian economy caused by the beginning of World War I.

It was also a time when conditions in North America were generally favorable. Industry was growing at a great pace, and there were openings even for those with few or no skills. Although the jobs might have paid little by North American standards, they were still more rewarding than those found in southern Italy.

The typical Italian immigrant to North America during this period was a young male with little formal education in his homeland and often speaking only broken English. Upon arrival, many immigrants were met by friends or relatives who had already made the trip and who provided a link to the new country, helping the new arrival become established in an Italian community where housing—usually in a crowded tenement—and work—most often manual labor—could be found. Later, when the immigrant had become more established and saved up enough money, he would arrange for others of his family, including his wife and children, to make the crossing. Unmarried immigrants were often matched up by relatives, who believed that the extended family offered the best protection in a new, and sometimes hostile, society.

THE FLOOD STOPS: WORLD WAR

Italian access to North America was eventually blocked by two developments. The first was World War I, which put a four-year halt to steamship travel across the Atlantic. After the war, immigration to the United States was severely limited by restrictive laws. The great number of persons entering the country had made those already living in the United States afraid that they would be "swamped" or "flooded" by outsiders.

This fear was aimed particularly at immigrants from eastern and southern Europe. Southern Italians generally had the characteristics of Mediterranean peoples: They were shorter, darker, and culturally different. Italian immigrants were further set apart because they spoke a foreign language and were predominantly Catholic.

All of these traits worked against Italians and other immigrants during a time when the United States, and to some extent Canada, were becoming increasingly "isolationist." Isolationism was a trend that developed after World War I: Many in America believed that they had enough troubles to worry about at home, in the United States and Canada, without having to worry about the economic and political troubles in Europe and the rest of the world. One expression of this isolationism was restrictive immigrant laws. America no longer needed immigrants to settle the frontier or build an industrial nation.

During the middle of the twentieth century, these laws and then World War II kept Italian arrivals in North America relatively low. It was not until the late 1940's that Italians in large numbers were again free to make North America their destination. Those who chose to make the trip did so for the same reasons earlier Italians had: bad conditions at home and better opportunities abroad. By 1958, more immigrants came to Canada from Italy than from Great Britain, the traditional primary source of people immigrating to Canada.

ITALIAN IMMIGRATION TODAY

In more recent years, the pace of immigration from Italy to North America has slowed, largely because of improvements in the economic and social conditions and opportunities in Italy. Today, Italy is a prosperous nation.

In a sense, the pattern of Italian immigration to North America has come full circle. The earliest immigrants crossed the ocean because of individual conditions, from a sense of adventure, or because they believed that they had the skills that would allow them to succeed in a new home. They were followed by a massive wave of immigrants who faced harsh prospects in Italy and believed that North America offered their best hope for a future. Since the 1960's, with Italy becoming a strong and economically powerful country, those who leave it do so largely for personal reasons.

WHEN THEY CAME

Italians have been coming to North America since Christopher Columbus in 1492. The flow of Italians to this continent, however, has not been a steady one.

There has been a definite pattern to Italian immigration to North America. For many years the number of Italians crossing the Atlantic was small. During the nineteenth century, immigration gradually increased but still remained modest. After the middle of the 1800's, there was a dramatic increase in the movement of Italians to North America. Then, after 1880, Italians began coming to this continent in considerable numbers.

Peak immigration occurred during the first two decades of the twentieth century. Then, Italian movement to North America was twice interrupted by world wars, from 1914 to 1918 and again from 1939 to 1945. When World War II ended, Italians had relatively free access to the United States and Canada, and immigration resumed. At this point, however, Italians did not come to North America in such large numbers as before. There was a steady, but much reduced, flow of immigrants.

EARLY IMMIGRATION: 1500-1800

From the time of Columbus to the time of Napoleon—that is, from roughly 1500 to 1800—very little changed in the life of the common Italian. The Italian peninsula was split, with a number of small, weak states and powerful foreign nations dividing the territory. No central government existed to finance any colonizing efforts. As a result, there were no Italian colonies in the New World, the way England, France, and Spain had colonies. If Italians wanted to move to North America, they had to do so on their own, as individuals.

The individual Italians who had the ability to make such a move lived mainly in the north of Italy. The north was the richer section of the peninsula, and its people were wealthier and better-educated. These people made up the majority of the few Italians who immigrated to North America, even until the middle of the 1800's.

Those who came during this period were artists, skilled workers, musicians, and teachers. Most of them did not flee grinding poverty. Instead, they were looking for better opportunity. Because of the difficulties in crossing the Atlantic during this time, these Italians needed sufficient resources, and courage, to make the difficult sea voyage.

For all these reasons, the flow was not very large. In the years between 1820 and 1850, for example, the number of Italian immigrants to the United States was not even five thousand. Very soon afterwards, however, that number increased, because, during the middle of the nineteenth century, conditions in Italy and the available means of travel both changed. Suddenly, in the decade between 1851 and 1860, the number of immigrants approach ten thousand.

FLEEING THE HOMELAND

In Italy, growing sentiment for national unification had led to increased political activity, and this activity was met by repressive measures from existing governments. Emigration increased after 1861: Many Italians who left during the 1860's and 1870's were escaping political persecution.

A second change in Italy was a growing awareness of the opportunities offered in North America. Word of the

economic, political, and social freedoms to be found in the
United States and Canada spread among the people, especially
those in southern Italy, where conditions were so bad. There
was a growing desire among Italians to find a better place to
live and raise their families, and North America seemed the
destination best suited to these goals.

Italians who had already made the move sent back money
and glowing stories of the new lands. Immigrants who had
already established themselves invited other members of their
family to join them. This phenomenon of "going to live with
the relatives in America" became known to North Americans
as "chain migration."

Boatloads of immigrants make the difficult Atlantic crossing.

THE AGE OF STEAM

A major reason for increased immigration was not only political but also technological. Crossing the Atlantic by sailing ship was slow, dangerous, and expensive. Sailing vessels could carry only a limited number of passengers and small amounts of cargo. Furthermore, because sailing ships were dependent upon the wind, shipping schedules were at the mercy of the seasons and weather. All of this made it difficult to move large groups of people.

With the development of the steamship, it became possible for larger numbers of passengers to make the Atlantic crossing relatively quickly and inexpensively. Larger vessels, a faster sailing time, and predictable schedules made mass immigration common. The trip was certainly very difficult, plagued by crowding, poor food, disease, and sometimes death. Many immigrants suffered extreme hardship during the journey, yet they were willing to withstand the trip in the hope of a better life than the one they had left. It was the steamship, more than any other single circumstance, that allowed for the dramatic increase in numbers of immigrants.

The results can be seen in the table. In the forty years from 1820 through 1860, less than 14,000 immigrants were recorded as arriving in the United States. During the single decade of 1861 through 1870, almost 12,000 Italians came to the United States. Then, in the next decade, this number jumped to nearly 56,000. The stage was set for a major increase in the number of Italians arriving in North America.

THE CREST OF THE WAVE: 1870 TO 1920

Italy was unified in 1870, and many Italians believed that their harsh economic and social situations would be relieved. Yet the new government largely ignored the plight of the peasants, and it did little to address the terrible conditions in the south of Italy. In many ways, already bad situations

41

became worse, and Italians were more willing to make the difficult choice of leaving their homeland.

Again, the results are seen in the statistics. In the decade after 1881, Italian immigration to the United States rose to more than 300,000 persons; most of these came from southern Italy. During the following ten years, the numbers more than doubled, exceeding 650,000. In the first decade of the twentieth century, an astounding number of Italians, more than two million, left Italy for America. This was the high-water mark of Italian immigration. During the next decade, the numbers were smaller, closer to one million, in part because World War I interrupted the exodus of Italians from the peninsula.

THE 1920'S AND AFTER

During the 1920's, the United States enacted restrictive immigration policies which slowed the influx of foreigners into the country. In large part these restrictive laws were enacted from fear of the enormous numbers of immigrants from eastern, central, and southern Europe, including Italy. By 1900, for example, one-fourth of the people in the United States were either foreign born or had a foreign-born parent.

In 1921 and 1924, the U.S. Congress enacted strict laws which placed a quota on the number of people who could come into the United States. The quota was set first at 3 percent, and then at 2 percent, of the total number of foreign-born people from each country counted in the 1890 census. Before these laws were enacted, people had been excluded from entering the United States only when they were considered unfit morally or medically or had a criminal record. These changes basically placed immigration on a first-come, first-served basis.

World War II brought another halt to immigration. With peace in 1945, the Italians were once again allowed the chance

Italian Immigration to the United States: 1820-1980

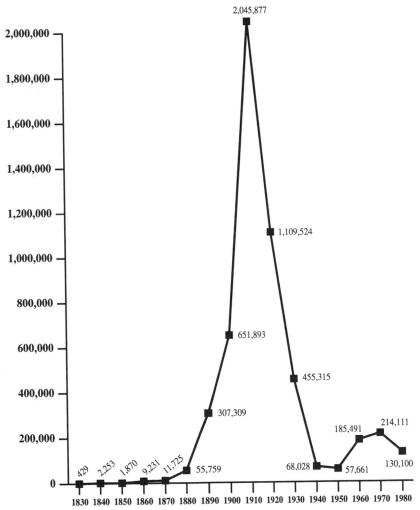

2,045,877

2,000,000

1,800,000

1,600,000

1,400,000

1,200,000

1,109,524

1,000,000

800,000

651,893

600,000

455,315

400,000

307,309

214,111

185,491

200,000

130,100

57,661

68,028

429 2,253 1,870 9,231 11,725 55,759

0

1830 1840 1850 1860 1870 1880 1890 1900 1910 1920 1930 1940 1950 1960 1970 1980

Sources: Nelli, Humbert S. *From Immigrants to Ethnics: The Italian Americans.* Oxford, England: Oxford University Press, 1983; Lerner, William, et al., *Historical Statistics of the United States, U.S. Statistical Abstracts.* Washington, D.C.: U.S. Government Printing Office, 1976.

to move to North America, but the number of those who chose to do so was significantly lower.

The reason for this was found, once again, in conditions in Italy. As Europe rebuilt from the ruins of war, with substantial aid from the United States' Marshall Plan, Italy became more prosperous and economically stable. Social conditions began to improve, even in the south. Italians who before might have migrated to find better jobs, greater freedom in politics, or more openness in social life now found these things in their homeland.

In other words, there were fewer reasons to leave Italy and more reasons to remain. Today, Italians who choose to leave do so for the same reasons that the first Italian immigrants did: to achieve personal goals, unique to themselves.

WHERE THEY LIVE

Before the great wave of immigrants that began in 1880, Italians could be found throughout the United States and Canada. Even during this early period, however, Italians in North America lived in or near major cities. In Canada, they concentrated around the area of Montreal and Quebec. In the United States, most Italians were found in the environs of New York and other northeastern cities, in New Orleans, or in the San Francisco region of California.

DECIDING WHERE TO SETTLE

There are three reasons for this geographical distribution. First, most Italian immigrants came to the United States through the ports of the Northeast, especially New York. When they found jobs, housing, and fellow Italians, they tended to remain.

Second, economic opportunity was greatest in the Northeast. During the time of peak Italian immigration, the Northeast was the section of the United States that was richest and most developed. With employment available and advancement possible, Italians had little reason to leave.

Third, Italians rapidly developed a sense of community. In other words, they made homes for themselves in their new country. Once established, they prospered far beyond what they could have dreamed of achieving in Italy.

For these reasons, Italians in North America for the most part became, and have remained, residents of large cities. It is in those areas that they have shared their talents and abilities with the other residents of their new homeland.

MAJOR NORTH AMERICAN CITIES

After 1880 the number of Italians arriving in North America greatly increased. Many of these new arrivals had been farmers or peasants in Italy, but when they arrived in Canada or the United States, they almost always lived in or near large cities. Most of these immigrants lived in the northeastern section of the United States, especially in the metropolitan New York area. In the years just before World War I, New York City had more Italians living there than Florence, Venice, and Genoa combined.

The major cities in this section of the United States became the homes for literally millions of Italians. Boston, Providence, Rhode Island, and the cities of New Jersey and Pennsylvania attracted a substantial Italian population. Well into the second half of the twentieth century, almost half of Italian Americans lived in the three states of New York, New Jersey, and Pennsylvania.

In Canada, Italian immigrants settled primarily in the large urban areas of Montreal and Toronto. Almost all Italian Canadians live in cities—approximately 95 percent—and they are also found in such important Canadian urban centers as Hamilton, St. Catharines, Windsor, Ottawa, Sault Ste. Marie, Calgary, and Edmonton.

In contemporary North America, persons of Italian descent still live mainly in the large urban areas. A change has taken place, however, in the sections of the cities in which they live. This change has taken place mainly because of the rising economic fortunes of Italian immigrants and their children and grandchildren.

The crowded Mulberry Street in New York City, 1909.

MIGRATION WITHIN THE CITIES

When the majority of Italian immigrants arrived in the United States and Canada, they were very poor, especially by North American standards. This was understandable, since they had come from the poorest section of Italy, the south. This poverty meant that the new arrivals had to find housing in the cheapest possible locations, and therefore they often lived first in slum areas. A great many immigrants existed in extremely bad conditions, crowded and unsanitary.

Since the immigrants from southern Italy had few skills that were marketable in a modern, industrial economy, and since they often spoke little or no English, their job opportunities were limited. They found work in factories, construction, and

47

transportation; women were employed in the garment industry. These jobs were generally located in the central parts of large cities, and Italians lived close to where they worked.

Italians tend to be close-knit and supporting of their countrymen, especially those from the same town or region, known in Italian as *paese*. Earlier immigrants to North America helped later arrivals find work and housing and aided them in adjusting to conditions in North America. Older and newer arrivals lived together in Italian communities within the cities. Such areas often came to be known as "Little Italies," because of their distinctly Italian character.

Economic and employment conditions thus channeled Italian immigrants into the inner city. Mulberry Street, a poor section of New York City occupied mainly by Italian immigrants, had some of the worst conditions in the entire country.

When the immigrants had the chance, they moved into better housing in neighborhoods, where they established a distinctive community of their own.

THE ITALIAN NEIGHBORHOOD

The most famous Little Italy is in New York City, but other examples are Brooklyn's Red Hook or Boston's North End. Red Hook was typical of many Italian-American communities because early immigrants settled there in large numbers for basic reasons: affordable, if crowded, living space, and available work. The neighborhood is located between Upper New York Bay and the Gowanus Bay, and this location made it suitable for shipping, shipbuilding, and related industries. Unskilled laborers could find employment as longshoremen, construction workers, and so forth.

The popular image of Red Hook became one of a tough, waterfront community which had associations with organized crime. To some extent this was true, partly because of living conditions which made the residents more trusting of each other than of authorities with whom they were still uncomfortable. In more recent years, Red Hook has shed much of this rougher image and has become more of a traditional Italian community, with close-knit, multigenerational families living in its numerous brownstone apartment houses. Many of the young men still find work on the docks and waterfront.

Most large cities of the northeastern United States have such Italian neighborhoods. Italian families have lived and worked in some of them for generations. In these neighborhoods are found Italian restaurants and shops which sell traditional foods and beverages of Italy. Italian traditions are preserved in these communities, including such festivals as that of San Gennaro in New York, or the feast of Our Lady of Mount Carmel, an annual event in Chicago's Melrose Park. The communities offer a sense of connection with fellow Italians and their descendants. At the same time, they have exposed non-Italians to many of the attractive and unique features of Italian life and culture.

The pattern of Italian neighborhoods in the United States was repeated in Canada, where the "Little Italy" section of Toronto is typical. Most Italian Canadians, like their counterparts to the south, live in cities and many of them actually came first to the United States, most often through New York, and then migrated a second time to Canada.

Italians made up about 10 percent of the total population of Toronto as recently as 1981, and many of these people still live together in their particular section of the city. Toronto's "Little Italy" is an ethnic community with the food stores, restaurants, social clubs and mutual benefit societies, and Roman Catholic churches found in such neighborhoods. However, Toronto's "Little Italy" is not rigidly separated from the rest of the city or its culture, but is an important part of the total metropolitan area. It still retains its special characteristics and is a distinct, vigorous, and economically viable part of the overall community.

In Montreal, where Italian Canadians make up more than 5 percent of the total population, the immigrants and their descendants have also created a relatively close-knit community, sometimes referred to as "Little Italy." Many of these residents are linked by family or regional connections, as well as by their common Italian heritage. The Italian population throughout Quebec generally is on excellent terms with the largely French-Canadian residents of the province, and intermarriage between the two groups is not uncommon. More than 80 percent of Italian Canadians speak French, which is very important in a province that is fiercely proud and protective of its French culture and identity.

SPREADING OUT

Greater geographical mobility came to Italians in North America after World War II. This was especially the case in the United States, where Italian-American veterans were able to take advantage of low-interest Veterans Administration loans and other programs offered by the federal government. These programs gave many Italian Americans the chance to own their first homes.

After World War II there was a shift of Italians away from the inner core of large cities. Many of them, along with many other Americans and Canadians, moved into the new suburbs that were growing up around the large cities. In both the United States and Canada, Italians and their descendants tended to remain close to the cities where they had first settled. In the United States, these were predominantly the urban areas of the Northeast. In Canada, Italians also moved into rural areas in the Niagara Peninsula, where many of them established orchards, vineyards, and truck farms.

WHERE THEY ARE TODAY

Even though the Italian Americans and Italian Canadians moved out of the central cities, they remained near them. In the United States, for example, more than 80 percent of Italian Americans live in what are called "standard metropolitan statistical areas," or SMSAs. These are regions defined by the U.S. Bureau of the Census and include large cities and the suburbs that surround them. Compared to the 80 percent of Italian Americans in SMSAs, only about 65 percent of all Americans live in such areas.

In the United States, these SMSAs are concentrated in the Northeast, where Italian Americans make up a large percentage of the total population. Italians are found especially in the areas around the major cities of Boston, Providence, New York, Philadelphia, and Pittsburgh. The situation is even more pronounced in Canada, where about 95 percent of Italian Canadians live in towns or cities. More than half of them, 65 percent, live in Ontario, and about a quarter of them (22 percent) live in Quebec.

Although a substantial number live in the Midwest, especially in the Chicago area, they comprise less than five percent of the total population in that region. In northern Minnesota, there is a fairly large concentration of Italian Americans who came to the area as farmers, often hired hands, and who remained.

The situation is even more marked in the south, where there are relatively few persons of Italian descent, except in the cities of Miami, Tampa, and New Orleans. New Orleans was an early center of Italian immigration.

In upstate New York, Italians made the effort to drain and farm rich lowlands south of Lake Ontario. They grew a variety of vegetables, especially onions, in these reclaimed fields. In general, however, Italian immigrants to North America tended to prefer city life to country life.

The landmark Catholic Church of St. Peter and St. Paul in the predominantly Italian American North Beach area of San Francisco, California.

There are some exceptions to the urban concentration of Italian Americans, but only a few. In the West, largely as an outgrowth of Italian immigration to San Francisco and the wine and truck farm areas, there are more Italians than are found in the South; still, they do not approach the numbers of this ethnic group in the Northeast. The valleys of California are probably the best-known non-urban areas where Italian immigrants and their descendants live. Italian Americans such as the Gallo brothers established winemaking in the Napa, Santa Clara, San Joaquin, and Sonoma valleys. In Colorado, north of New Mexico, concentrations of Italians can be found as a result of laborers who came to the area to work on the railroads and, later, to work as miners. Where the land permitted, many of these Italians later became farmers and ranchers.

For the most part, however, Italian Americans and their descendants remain an urban group, despite their predominantly agricultural heritage.

WHAT THEY DO

The jobs that Italian immigrants found in North America were often determined by their place of origin in Italy. Those who came from northern Italy were generally better-educated and so had the skills needed for professions that required practice in the crafts or arts. Southern Italians, on the other hand, were predominantly peasant farmers, or *contadini*, who arrived with few marketable skills and found that they had to take whatever jobs were available—generally those in low-paying manual labor or factory work.

ARTISTS AND ARTISANS

This geographical and social distinction was clear from the earliest days of Italian immigration. Before the later part of the 1800's, the majority of immigrants from the peninsula came from the north. They included artists (sculptors, painters, and musicians), teachers, skilled craftspersons such as glass workers and furniture makers, and merchants or traders who established small businesses.

During this first part of Italian immigration, the typical Italian in North America was employed in a profession or trade that required a fairly high degree of skill and education. In Canada, for example, Italians were very active in the hotel and restaurant industry, particularly in the larger cities. In the United States, many early Italian immigrants found work as teachers of music or art, or practiced themselves as artists. Many of the artworks of the United States Capitol building,

An Italian-American stonecutter hard at work in Barre, Vermont.

for example, were fashioned by Constantino Brumidi, a native of Italy, who worked in Washington, D.C., from 1855 until his death in 1877.

Until 1880, Italians who came to North America almost universally fit into this pattern. Relatively few in number, usually educated and skilled, they settled in the cities and blended well into existing society. In most cases they were respected for the talents that they had brought to their new homeland.

PEASANT FARMERS AND UNSKILLED LABORERS

This situation changed dramatically after 1880. That year marked a shift in both the numbers and the backgrounds of the Italians immigrating to North America. Starting in 1880, much larger numbers of Italians crossed the Atlantic, and the vast majority of them were from southern Italy.

This second wave of immigrants was drawn from the middle or lower economic classes, especially from the peasantry. They thus had fewer skills than earlier immigrants. Because of the harsh conditions in southern Italy, many of these arrivals had little education, and often they were illiterate.

For all of these reasons, and because of the anti-immigrant prejudices of persons already living in North America, Italians arriving after 1880 received a cooler reception and found their opportunities of employment limited. Most of them could find work only as manual laborers: in factories, construction, transportation, or farming.

Quite a few Italians were recruited in Italy for passage to North America by labor bosses. The boss, known as a *padrone*, signed contracts with farmers and companies in the United States and Canada to bring over work crews. While many of these bosses were honest and fair, some of them were interested only in profits and took advantage of the peasant immigrants by cheating them of their wages or leaving them stranded and unemployed in the major cities of Canada and the United States. Even when the *padrone* was honorable, the work was hard and the wages were low.

TAKING ADVANTAGE OF OPPORTUNITY

Still, conditions in North America were better than those in Italy. The Italian workers sent money home to their families in the old country, and with their money went word of the possibility of a better life in Canada or the United States. Literally millions of Italians decided to cross the ocean. Entire families made the passage, often in a serial fashion, as earlier immigrants became established and Italian relatives followed.

These newcomers typically remained in the large cities of the East Coast. They went to work in factories or manufacturing or construction. Women entered the garment industry, sewing and making clothes. By the early years of the twentieth century, Italian women had become the largest single group of laborers in the garment industry.

Although Italians began in such jobs, they did not always remain in them. Hardworking and industrious, Italian immigrants were determined to become more economically secure and better educated. As they did, they were able to move into other businesses. A number of them became successful in the import trade, specializing in the cheeses, oil, and wine that their fellow countrymen—and, in time, many non-Italians—desired.

FOOD, FARMING, FISHING

Food became a particular avenue of success for Italians. At first they opened restaurants to serve themselves and the residents of Italian neighborhoods. Then, as other Canadians and Americans learned the delicious attraction of Italian cuisine, these restaurants found patrons from the larger

A delicatessen display, common to any "Little Italy" across North America, includes spaghetti, cannoli, ravioli, stewed tomatoes, salami, olive oil, and more.

community. Today there are Italian restaurants throughout North America.

On the West Coast, opportunities discovered by Italian immigrants were somewhat different from those on the East Coast. Italians who settled in California, for example, recognized that the fertile soil and favorable climate were perfect for raising fruits and vegetables. These crops could be shipped to markets in nearby cities by truck, so the operations came to be known as "truck farms."

One Italian who was vastly successful at truck farming was Marco Fontana, a native of Genoa who settled in California. In 1891, Fontana founded a company known as Del Monte, which later became famous for its canned fruits and vegetables. Today, Del Monte is part of the California Packing

58

Company, the largest fruit and vegetable canning company in the world.

West Coast Italians also introduced the wine industry to North America. The Gallo brothers, Ernest and Julio, as well as other vintners, discovered that the Sonoma Valley was the perfect location for growing wine grapes. They used their skills to build a business empire which brought a new appreciation for the winemaker's art to American culture, and to a large extent laid the groundwork for the winemaking industry in the United States.

In seacoast cities, Italians also became active in commercial fishing, a natural outgrowth of that occupation in Italy. They were successful on the East Coast, in places such as Boston, Massachusetts, and Providence, Rhode Island. They were found in the South, in Tampa, Florida, and New Orleans, Louisiana. Their greatest success, however, was in the San Francisco area, where by 1910 they were responsible for an astounding 80 percent of the commercial fish catch.

FROM WORKER TO PROFESSIONAL

The work that Italians do in North America has changed over the years. Many of them are still found in jobs in labor, manufacturing, restaurants, and commercial fishing. More and more, however, as the Italian Americans and Italian Canadians have moved into the mainstream of North American society, they have gained the education and skills to occupy a variety of roles.

In contemporary North America, Italians and their descendants can be found in all walks of life. They are lawyers, doctors, bankers, entrepreneurs, farmers, industrialists, and artists. At one time the typical Italian in North America was restricted to a low-paying job in manual labor. Today, he or she is a dramatic representative of the opportunity available to those with drive and determination.

CONTRIBUTIONS TO

SOCIETY

All immigrant groups have added to the rich mix and diversity of life in North America. The variety that is a hallmark of this continent is a legacy of immigration, for those who came here brought their own traditions to expand the horizons of those already settled here. Among these immigrant groups, Italians have made some of the most notable contributions to their new homeland. The millions of Italians who have arrived on these shores gave birth to many who became famous in various fields, and there have also been countless numbers of anonymous Italians who have left an indelible imprint upon North America.

ART AND ARCHITECTURE

The earliest Italian immigrants brought with them a rich and important legacy of culture and art. Not only were many of them artists, scholars, and musicians themselves; they also introduced North America to the glories of Italy's rich cultural heritage.

During the early years of the United States, men such as Thomas Jefferson, the author of the Declaration of Independence and the new nation's third president, were greatly influenced by Italian accomplishments in architecture and design. Jefferson's own plans for his beloved home,

Monticello, clearly demonstrate this, for the house shows unmistakable traces of the clear, flowing lines of Italian Renaissance forms. In fact, the name Jefferson chose for his home is itself Italian, and means "little mountain."

The capital of the United States, Washington, D.C., is in many ways an Italian city in design, because so many of its public buildings are based upon architecture perfected during the great days of the Roman Republic. This was a conscious choice, because the early American republic looked upon the ancient Roman state as the best example of a successful and enduring government of free citizens.

The dome of the American Capitol and the columns and facades of the Supreme Court building and other federal structures have their origin in Roman architecture. Even the choice of the American eagle as the national symbol of the United States was greatly influenced by the Roman eagle.

Italian painting and sculpture have also had a great impact upon those arts in North America. American artists from the early days of the nation often made extended visits to Italy to study painting there. Many of them brought back skills and techniques that contributed to the growth and development of American art. Contemporary painters of Italian descent continue in this tradition. Museums and galleries throughout the United States and Canada house masterpieces of such Italian-American artists, as well as masterpieces from Italy.

MUSIC AND OPERA

Another Italian cultural contribution to North America has been opera, that combination of drama and music that many people believe to be the highest form of artistic expression. One of the first Italians to come to the newly founded United States was Lorenzo da Ponte, a multitalented genius who wrote the words, or *libretto*, to the famous opera *The Marriage of Figaro*, for which Wolfgang Amadeus Mozart

61

composed the music. Other Italians—singers, directors, and musicians—encouraged this interest in opera. In 1847, the Astor Place Opera House became the first hall devoted to Italian opera in New York City.

These contributions in the areas known as the "fine arts" have continued into contemporary times. In 1976, the famous Italian composer Gian Carlo Menotti chose Charleston, South Carolina, as the site of the internationally renowned Spoleto Festival. Every year, famous musicians and performing artists gather in Charleston to present a mixture of opera, drama, concerts, exhibits, street festivals, and other arts. The Spoleto Festival has become one of the major artistic events in the world, attracting thousands of spectators each spring.

William Struhs

Gian Carlo Menotti, founder and Artistic Director of the Spoleto Festival in Charleston, South Carolina.

LITERATURE AND FILM

During the nineteenth century, cultivated Italian immigrants brought the magnificence of Italian literature to North America, and American and Canadian writers were awed by the power of this writing, especially Dante Alighieri's *Divine Comedy*, one of the most important poems of the early Italian Renaissance. In more modern times, the American poet Ezra Pound was deeply affected by Italian writing. He based many of his own works on Italian sources or inspirations. The noted American poet John Ciardi, of Italian descent, wrote much excellent original verse, and his translation of Dante's *Divine Comedy* is recognized as one of the finest.

Italian Americans have also been concerned with expressing the Italian immigrant's experience in North America. The author Mario Puzo saw his novel *The Godfather* (1969) become a best-seller and in 1972 an Academy Award-winning motion picture. Both the book and the film (and sequels to the film) portray an Italian-American crime family and, in the process, depict much about the attitudes toward family, life, and relationships—between men and women, parents and children—that many viewers recognized as deeply Italian. The film was directed by an Italian American, the talented Francis Ford Coppola, one of the most original of modern filmmakers.

Frank Capra, another Italian American whose movies have become classics, directed such films as *Mr. Smith Goes to Washington*, *It's a Wonderful Life*, and the outstanding series *Why We Fight*, which reinforced public morale during World War II. At the heart of each of these films are issues concerning what it means to be an American.

Italian Americans have been among the greatest of actors and entertainers: Jimmy Durante, Liza Minelli, Tony Bennett, and the legendary Frank Sinatra have left an enduring mark on world culture. Their fine performances, films, and recordings have given pleasure to millions.

SPORTS

In the field of sports, Italians have shown exceptional ability. Even a quick glance at the record books shows how many championship teams have depended upon the skills and talents of their players of Italian descent. Nowhere is this more evident than in the American national pastime, baseball: Players such as Yogi Berra, Phil Rizutto, Dolph Camilli, Rocky Colavito, and Tony Conigliaro are among the most outstanding players in the history of the game. One of the greatest players ever was Joe DiMaggio of the New York Yankees, whose fifty-six-game hitting streak in 1941 remains one of baseball's most enduring records. Among more recent players, Joe Garagiola became well known first as an outstanding catcher for the St. Louis Cardinals and then as a noted television personality. Tommy Lasorda, long-time manager of the Los Angeles Dodgers, led his team to World Series victories in 1981 and 1988.

Italian Americans and Italian Canadians have been quite successful in other sports. Phil Esposito was one of the most skillful hockey players of his time and helped the Boston Bruins to win the Stanley Cup in 1967. Mario Andretti, born in Italy and a naturalized American, became well known for his success in world-class automobile racing. Horse racing was the path which Eddie Arcaro followed, and the jockey was elected to his sport's hall of fame in 1955.

Football is another sport in which Italians have excelled, and no one demonstrated this better than Vince Lombardi, longtime coach of the Green Bay Packers. Lombardi coached the Packers to five National Football League championships and led them to victory in the first two Super Bowl games. He was elected to the Football Hall of Fame in 1972.

POLITICS

Italians have made important contributions to American

political life since the very early days. Philip Mazzei, an Italian immigrant who settled in Virginia in 1773, was a friend of Thomas Jefferson. Mazzei may well have influenced Jefferson's draft of the Declaration of Independence, which seems to echo an earlier essay by Mazzei which states: "All men are by nature equally free and independent." These words sound very similar to Jefferson's famous statement, "All men are created equal."

Another notable Italian leader during the early years of the American nation was William Paca, who was a member of the Continental Congress and a signer of the Declaration of Independence. Paca was later elected to the Maryland State Senate and as governor of that state, serving three terms from 1782 to 1785. He was also a state and federal judge.

In more recent years, Italian Americans have achieved distinction in government. Fiorello La Guardia served in the U.S. House of Representatives from 1917 to 1921 and again from 1923 to 1933, when he was elected mayor of New York City. He was an immensely popular mayor and served for three terms. John O. Pastore, who had served as governor of Rhode Island during the mid-1940's, became the first Italian American to be elected to the U.S. Senate, in 1950. In 1984, Geraldine Ferraro became the first woman and first Italian American nominated for vice president of the United States by a major political party, the Democrats.

BUSINESS

Italians have also made significant contributions in the area of business. Italians immigrated to North America because they rightly believed it to be a land of opportunity. Many of them transformed that promise into performance.

In doing so, they created new markets for business, especially in food and beverages. Italians who settled in California led in developing the truck-farm industry, harvesting and canning crops of fruits and vegetables for distribution throughout the nation. The well-known Del Monte company, founded in 1891 by Marco J. Fontana, has become part of the largest canning company in the world.

In Canada, Italians also made their mark in business, including Onorato Catelli of Montreal, who was very successful in the food-processing industry. Because many Italian Canadians had started in construction and transportation, these were areas in which they excelled. Vincent Franceschini of Toronto, for example, became well known in road construction. Two Italian-Canadian brothers who began as ordinary laborers, Vincenzo and Giovanni Veltri, established the Welch Construction Company around 1900. Their company was a major handler of maintenance for the extensive Canadian railway system.

PIZZA, PASTA, PROSCIUTTO

Food and drink are the means by which Italians have made their most widespread mark on North American culture. Many people appreciate art and literature, but all of us respond to food, and North Americans have eagerly adopted the cuisine of Italy, making Italian dishes among the most popular ethnic foods in Canada and the United States.

Pizza, lasagna, spaghetti, veal, and scampi are some of the more notable foods introduced by Italians into North America. These dishes are quite familiar today, and pizza has become a universal favorite: It has become so popular and so "mass-produced," in fact, that pizza is now more American than it is Italian. Yet, as recently as the beginning of the twentieth century, these foods were almost unknown by the majority of Americans.

Italians, in particular southern Italians, brought these foods with them. They also brought the rich mixture of ingredients which make these delicious items. Highly flavored tomato sauce is a southern Italian staple, and there are also the wonderful range of cheeses, such as mozzarella, ricotta, romano, and parmesan. There are the Italian meats, such as salami, Italian sausage, and prosciutto, or Italian ham. Blended with herbs such as garlic, basil, and oregano, these have become familiar favorites of millions.

Robert Mondavi Winery, Oakville, CA

Robert Mondavi

Without a doubt, the centerpiece of Italian-American cooking is pasta, a dried mixture of flour and water which is both nutritious and easy to store. The variety of pasta shapes and forms which the Italians have given to North America are almost endless. Some of them are quite familiar, such as elbow macaroni, vermicelli, manicotti, fettucine, or ravioli. Others are more exotic, such as the "little shells," or conchiglie, and "pen tips," or mostaccioli. Each type of pasta is shaped differently, raising the making of pasta to an art.

In more recent years, the robust flavor of southern Italian cooking has been supplemented by the introduction of northern Italian dishes. These are generally lighter and less highly flavored, relying much less on tomato sauce in their preparation. Among the most famous examples of this northern Italian cuisine are veal piccata, flavored with lemon juice. This dish can also be made with chicken or pork. While these choices may never replace pizza or spaghetti as popular favorites, they have brought a little more of Italy to North American meals.

Finally, Italian immigrants introduced an entire industry to North America: winemaking. This multibillion-dollar enterprise was developed by such successful entrepreneurs as Ernest and Julio Gallo and Robert Mondavi, who cultivated outstanding varieties of grapes in the favorable California climate and then used their skills to produce wines which are the equal to any found in Europe. Their success has brought a greater sophistication in American dining.

FAMOUS ITALIAN

AMERICANS

Italian immigrants and their descendants have made lasting and important contributions to life in the United States and Canada. These contributions have come in many areas, including politics, business, science, entertainment, and literature.

MOTHER CABRINI, SAMARITAN AND SAINT

Frances Xavier Cabrini, best known as Mother Cabrini, was the first American citizen to be canonized as a saint by the Roman Catholic church. Her exemplary life began in 1850, when she was born in the small Italian town of Sant' Angelo, in the area near Milan. She was the youngest of thirteen children.

She became a teacher and tried to become a nun with the order of the Daughters of the Sacred Heart, but she was rejected because of her frail health. The Canossians, another religious order, denied her application for the same reason. In 1874 she went to work with a small orphanage, the House of Providence, and in 1877 she became directress of the institution, taking her religious vows at that time.

On November 14, 1880, Frances Cabrini and seven other sisters started the Missionary Sisters of the Sacred Heart. The order was dedicated to serving Italian immigrants in North and

69

South America. In 1889, Mother Cabrini landed in New York City and began to supervise the activities of the order's headquarters there personally.

Throughout her lifetime, Mother Cabrini established orphanages, nurseries, hospitals, and schools in the United States, and opened religious houses in the United States, France, England, Nicaragua, Argentina, and Brazil. In all, sixty-seven establishments were created. The Sisters of the Sacred Heart were especially concerned with the plight of the poor, taking special pains to provide medical care and educational opportunities to the children of Italian immigrants.

Mother Cabrini died on December 22, 1917, in Chicago. In 1946, she was declared a saint through canonization by the Catholic church. Her feast day is observed on November 13.

BANKING ON AMERICA: AMADEO PETER GIANNINI

Many Italian Americans have left permanent and impressive contributions to American and Canadian business and industry, but few have matched the mark set by Amadeo Peter Giannini.

Born in San José, California, in 1870, Giannini started work at age twelve in the San Francisco produce company owned by his stepfather. By age nineteen, Giannini had become a full partner in the business. Through his experience he learned the importance of banks and the loans they could offer to small and growing businesses. In 1904, he started his own financial institution, the Bank of Italy. The new bank had only $150,000 in capital, which was a small sum even for those days.

Giannini's Bank of Italy grew rapidly because it served a share of the market that had been largely ignored by other banks: the small businessman, first-time homeowners, and families earning modest incomes. The bank quickly rebounded from the famous 1906 San Francisco earthquake and led the way in providing funds for the city to rebuild.

Giannini brought innovations and improvements to the

Amadeo Peter Giannini

banking industry. He introduced branch banking to California in 1909. His bank was the first to grant home loans that could be repaid in small, monthly installments. This made it possible, for the first time, for thousands of families to own a home.

The Bank of Italy also pioneered the practice of granting loans on modest collateral. Collateral is the property or goods that a person uses to "secure" a loan. If the person is unable to repay the loan to the bank, the bank can take the collateral in order to recover the money it lent. By requiring only a small amount of collateral, Giannini could give badly needed help to small businesses, which required ready money in order to expand and grow. These loans were extremely important to many immigrants seeking to establish new businesses in North America.

In 1928, Giannini founded the Transamerica Corporation, which incorporated his original bank and many other operations. The name of the bank changed to the Bank of America. At the time Giannini died in 1949, the Transamerica Corporation was the largest private banking system in the world. Today, it remains an economic giant and includes many other concerns besides banking.

FIORELLO LA GUARDIA, MAYOR OF NEW YORK

Italian Americans have been active in government and politics for a long time. Their emergence into the political limelight, however, did not really take place until well into the twentieth century. One of the most notable and colorful of Italian-American political leaders was Fiorello Henry La Guardia.

La Guardia was born in New York City in 1882, but his father died soon after, and young Fiorello was sent to live with relatives in Europe. He grew up in what is now Hungary, and when he was still a young man he began working with the United States foreign service in Italy. By the time he was twenty-one years old, he had been appointed acting U.S. consul in the cities of Fiume and Trieste, in northern Italy.

In 1907, La Guardia returned to New York City and soon entered politics. He was elected to Congress in 1916. During World War I, he was a bomber pilot on the Italian front. Upon his return to the United States he was again active in government, serving in the United States House of Representatives from 1917 to 1921 and again from 1923 to 1933.

Elected as a Republican, La Guardia soon broke ranks with that party and allied himself with the Democrats and progressive members of Congress. He was a strong supporter of the rights of working men and women, and he fought for legislation that protected the rights of workers, especially in their union activities.

In 1933, La Guardia was elected the ninety-ninth mayor of New York City. He served three terms, from 1934 through 1945, and could easily have won a fourth time but decided not to run. During his tenure as mayor, La Guardia was vigorous in building projects to improve New York, including parks, bridges, tunnels, and housing units. A friendly and outgoing man, he was nicknamed "The Little Flower" by the people he served.

La Guardia's term as mayor was of great benefit to the city. He was able to work with both Democrats and Republicans in governing the metropolis, and his close connection with the people of New York was unsurpassed. He was truly a representative of the best Italian Americans had to offer their chosen country.

FRANK CAPRA, FILMMAKER

Motion pictures have been seen by many people as a distinctly American contribution to world culture, and one of the most accomplished and popular of American film directors was Frank Capra. His most successful motion pictures combine a strong faith in the basic strength and goodness of common people with a positive view of American life.

Capra was born in Palermo, Sicily, in 1897, and he came to the United States in 1903. He began his career in Hollywood in the early 1920's, but it was during the 1930's and 1940's that he made his most famous movies.

Capra had a special touch with comedies that also had a sentimental tone, touching the feelings of the audience while making them laugh. *It Happened One Night* (1934) is regarded as a landmark in American film, while *Mr. Deeds Goes to Town* (1936) and *You Can't Take It With You* (1938) were both critical and popular successes. For all three of these films, Capra won the Academy Award for Best Director.

Political movies, most notably *Mr. Smith Goes to Washington* (1939) and *Meet John Doe* (1941), were also part of Capra's work. In these films, he showed how common, everyday Americans used truth and justice to defeat lies and injustice. During World War II, Capra was responsible for the stirring series *Why We Fight*, which brilliantly presented the reasons America and its allies waged war against Nazi Germany and its partners.

Capra's most famous and typical movie is probably *It's A Wonderful Life* (1946), a combination of comedy, sentiment, and celebration of everyday American life starring Jimmy Stewart and Donna Reed. Stewart plays a small-town banker who struggles against a corrupt business and political boss, becoming disillusioned with life when he is unable to defeat these forces of evil. On the verge of taking his own life, he discovers—through the help of a comic angel named Clarence—that even a "little guy" like him is important, and he goes on to defeat the evil forces plaguing his small town. The film's humor, combined with its hopeful, positive message, have made it a favorite of audiences over the years.

EXPLORING THE ATOM: ENRICO FERMI

Enrico Fermi, born and reared in Italy, became a naturalized citizen of the United States and one of the outstanding figures in modern science. He won the Nobel Prize for his work in physics and was one of the team that developed the atom bomb during World War II. Without Fermi, the United States and its allies might have lost the desperate race to produce this ultimate weapon.

Born in Rome, Italy, in 1901, Fermi was a brilliant student and later an outstanding teacher. Fermi studied and absorbed the breakthroughs in physics which were taking place during the early years of the twentieth century, and he built upon them. During the 1930's, he conducted extensive experiments on radioactivity in his laboratory in Rome. It was during this time that he made important discoveries about the atom and

The Nobel Foundation

Enrico Fermi

atomic reactions, for which he won the 1938 Nobel Prize in Physics.

It was also during this time that Italy fell completely under the control of Benito Mussolini and his Fascist Party. The Fascists and their tyranny were clearly understood and despised by Fermi, and when he realized that he could no longer resist them, he emigrated to the United States.

Fermi continued his study of physics, especially radioactivity, in the United States. When World War II erupted, he was part of the top-secret Manhattan Project, consisting of a group of scientists who developed the atomic bomb. It was Fermi who supervised the team that first produced a successful nuclear chain reaction, the key element needed for a working bomb.

Later, when the project was based in Los Alamos, New Mexico, Fermi was largely responsible for solving difficult problems that none of the other scientists could unravel. Although all involved were important, Enrico Fermi was indispensable.

FRANK SINATRA: SINGER, ACTOR

Italian Americans have traditionally been associated with music, but probably no single performer has had such a lasting career as Frank Sinatra. For many years, Sinatra was not only a dominant force in American popular song but an international celebrity as well. He also enjoyed success as an outstanding actor in motion pictures.

Sinatra was born in 1915, in Hoboken, New Jersey. After becoming well known locally, he burst upon the national scene during the early 1940's. His concerts were notable for the great excitement they caused among his fans, especially teenage girls, known as "bobby soxers." Sinatra was the first great singer to generate the frenzy that later groups, such as the Beatles, would one day inspire.

76

Frank Sinatra

As a singer, Sinatra displayed a remarkably wide range in his material. He could perform equally well in fast, up-tempo numbers, light romantic songs, and tender ballads. He was able to create a mood and atmosphere with his voice and presence that captivated his audiences. His dramatic singing powers are best displayed in the tune most closely associated with him, "My Way."

Sinatra's popularity led him to films, where his dramatic abilities allowed him to excel. Of course, he was sometimes cast in musicals, such as *Anchors Aweigh* (1945) or *High Society* (1956), the musical remake of the comedy *The Philadelphia Story*. However, Sinatra's best roles were in more serious films.

From Here to Eternity (1953) was a startling break for Sinatra, in which he impressed audiences and critics with his skillful handling of a difficult and challenging role. He was also remarkably effective in the dark political thriller *The Manchurian Candidate* (1962), which was not shown in theaters for several years because of its plot's eerie similarities to the circumstances surrounding the assassination of President John F. Kennedy in 1963. Sinatra was also cast in a number of detective films, in which he generally played a cynical but essentially honest cop.

It is as a singer, however, that Frank Sinatra is best known and will best be remembered. His accomplishments in that field are without equal among his contemporaries. He was the first, for example, to make a long-playing record album in which all the songs were designed to work together to inspire a particular mood.

FRANK PACI, MARIO PUZO: WRITING THE ITALIAN-AMERICAN EXPERIENCE

Literature has always been a rich field for Italian immigrants, and many distinguished and skillful writers have addressed the experience of their countrymen in a new land. A number of powerful novels have been written using this theme.

One Canadian writer who has explored the immigrant life is Frank Gilbert Paci. He was born in Pesaro, Italy, in 1948, but came to Canada in 1952. Paci attended the University of Toronto and Carleton University, and in addition to writing he also taught.

Paci's writing is concerned with ethnic identity, the traits and experiences that are shared by the Italian-Canadian community. He is also interested in personal self-discovery— that is, how the individual grows and matures as a unique, original person. These two themes are found throughout his works, including *The Italians* (1978), *The Father* (1984), and *Black Madonna* (1982).

The Italian-American novelist Mario Puzo is also concerned with these themes, and as a result his novels have been hailed by critics. Puzo was born in New York City in 1920. His father was a railroad worker, and as a young man Mario was also employed by the railroads. He was in the United States Air Force during World War II, serving as a public relations officer in Europe after that conflict had ended.

Returning to civilian life, Puzo worked as an editor on several magazines, did free-lance writing, and continued to perfect his fiction. Two of his earlier books, *Dark Arena* (1955) and *The Fortunate Pilgrim* (1965), were praised by critics as sensitive, well-written studies of Italian immigrants and their lives in the United States.

Puzo's greatest success came in 1969, when he published *The Godfather*. This novel is the sweeping epic of mafia don Vito Corleone and became a huge best-seller. So successful was it, in fact that it became the basis for an entire series of motion pictures, with Puzo collaborating on the screenplays for *The Godfather* (1972), *The Godfather Part II* (1974), and *The Godfather Part III* (1990).

ARTISTS: GUIDO MOLINARI AND FRANK STELLA

Guido Molinari has been an important influence on Canadian art. Born in Montreal in 1933, he received his training at the School of Design at the Montreal Museum of Fine Arts. Later, Molinari became both a painter and a teacher of younger artists.

Molinari's style combines the principles of abstract art with a careful, disciplined technique. This gives his work a unique and challenging look. His accomplishments have been widely recognized. In 1968, he won the David E. Bright Foundation Prize at the Biennale in Venice, Italy. In 1980, the Quebec government honored him with the Paul-Émile Bordua Prize.

An Italian-American artist who has been important in the twentieth century is Frank Stella, born in 1936 in Malden, Massachusetts. Stella attended the Phillips Exeter Academy and later was graduated from Princeton University with a degree in fine art. His education introduced him to the works of modern masters who influenced his style. He was especially impressed with the geometrical patterns used by the painter Piet Mondrian. These influences are clearly seen in Stella's canvases.

After graduating from Princeton, Stella supported himself by painting houses, while he continued his own creative work. His paintings were recognized as powerful statements, and in 1960 he was given an exhibition at the famous Museum of Modern Art in New York City.

Stella's paintings have a look that is unmistakably his own. He uses flat, very defined shapes, especially stripes. Often these geometrical patterns are brightly colored. Stella's purpose is to make the viewer focus on the painting and its contents as pure objects, rather than as representations of something else. This emphasis on the painting *as* a painting is very important in modern art, and Frank Stella is one of its most prominent champions.

REACHING FOR HIGH OFFICE: GERALDINE FERRARO

In 1984, when Geraldine Anne Ferraro ran on the Democratic ticket with Walter Mondale, she became the first woman nominated for vice president of the United States by a major political party. Her nomination was a result of years of political achievements.

Born in 1935 in Newburgh, New York, Geraldine Ferraro was the daughter of an Italian immigrant. Her father died when Geraldine was only eight, and she was reared mainly by her mother. In later years, Ferraro would retain her maiden

Democratic National Committee

Geraldine Ferraro speaking at the 1984 Democratic National Convention, in San Francisco.

name, wishing to honor the memory of the astounding sacrifices made by her mother.

A 1956 graduate of Marymount Manhattan College, Ferraro taught English in the public schools and attended Fordham University to earn a law degree in 1960. That same year, she married John Zaccaro; the couple had three children.

Active for many years in community and civic affairs, Ferraro was appointed assistant district attorney of New York in 1974 and was successful in prosecuting a number of cases, often involving crimes against women, the elderly, or children. In 1978, she won a congressional seat from the Queens borough of New York City, and she was easily reelected in 1978 and 1980.

A hardworking and conscientious member of the House of Representatives, Ferraro soon became a recognized leader in the national Democratic Party. She was an eloquent and articulate spokesperson for social and economic causes, but she tempered her approach with realism.

In 1984, the Democratic Party's nominee for president of the United States, Walter Mondale, chose Geraldine Ferraro as his running mate. Throughout the campaign, Representative Ferraro excited great interest and admiration for her poise and presence, and, although the Democrats lost the presidential election, many observers were favorably impressed with Ferraro's style and substance.

TIME LINE

1492	Columbus discovers the New World.
1497	Giovanni Caboto (John Cabot) explores the coast of Canada.
1499	Amerigo Vespucci explores the coasts of South America and announces that a new continent has been discovered.
1524	Giovanni da Verrazzano explores the North American coast.
1620's	Italian artisans arrive in the English colonies.
1678	Henri de Tonty arrives in North America with La Salle.
1682	Tonty and La Salle explore the Mississippi River.
1702	Father Eusebio Francisco Kino explores the southwestern portion of North America, including modern-day California and Arizona, building more than thirty churches and chapels.
1773	Philip Mazzei, Italian political philosopher and friend of Thomas Jefferson, arrives in Virginia.
1776	William Paca, member of the Continental Congress, signs the Declaration of Independence.
1805	Lorenzo da Ponte, librettist of *The Marriage of Figaro*, arrives in America.
1812-1814	200 Italian mercenaries fight for Great Britain in the War of 1812. They take up lands granted by the British government in Canada.
1820-1840	Only fourteen thousand Italians settle in the United States.
1825	The first Italian opera to be performed in New York City, *The Barber of Seville*, is mounted.
1847	Astor Place Opera House is built in New York City; it is the first devoted to Italian opera.
1855	Constantino Brumidi is employed to decorate the United States Capitol.
1861	Gaetano Lanza establishes the Massachusetts Institute of Technology.
1861	The Garibaldi Guard is formed in New York City; it fights for the Union throughout the American Civil War.

1870	The unification of Italy is complete when Rome and Venetia join Italy.
1880	Italians begin to immigrate to North America in large numbers.
1880	*Il Progresso Italo-Americano*, an Italian newspaper, is established in New York City.
1881	Two thousand people of Italian origin live in Canada, principally in Montreal and Toronto.
1886	The Italian publication *Italia* is established in Chicago.
1887	Francis B. Spinola is elected to the House of Representatives from New York, the first Italian American to hold this seat in federal government.
1888	The first mention of the Mafia appears in the American press.
1889	Frances Xavier Cabrini (Mother Cabrini) arrives in New York to lead the Missionary Sisters of the Sacred Heart.
1891	Eleven Italians are murdered by the mob in New Orleans, causing an international scandal.
1892	Mother Cabrini opens Columbus Hospital in New York City.
1904	Amadeo Giannini founds the Bank of Italy in California, later renamed the Bank of America.
1905	The Order of the Sons of Italy is founded.
1906	Amadeo Obici founds the Planters Peanuts company.
1907	The peak year of Italian immigration to the United States: 285,731 Italian immigrants arrive.
1912	The Lawrence Textile Strike, in Lawrence, Massachusetts, demonstrates the importance of Italian organized labor in the United States.
1913	The first branch of the Order of Italy in founded in Sault Ste. Marie, Canada.
1917	The first laws in restricting immigration into the United States are passed.
1921	The United States enacts more restrictive immigration laws.
1921	Nicola Sacco and Bartolomo Vanzetti are convicted of murder— victims of prejudice against Italians in the United States.
1923	Gaetano Merola founds the San Francisco Opera Company.
1924	The United States enacts the Johnson-Reed Act, placing restrictions on immigration.
1926	The Order of Italo-Canadians is established in Quebec.
1927	Sacco and Vanzetti are executed.
1930	More Italians live in New York City than in Rome, Italy.

1933   Fiorello Henry La Guardia is elected mayor of New York City.

1936   Enrico Fermi, one of the key scientists to develop the atomic bomb, emigrates to the United States.

1936   Joe DiMaggio joins the New York Yankees; during his career (1936-1951), he has a .325 lifetime average and hits 361 home runs.

1938   Hubert Badanai of Fort William (now Thunder Bay) becomes the first Canadian mayor of Italian descent.

1939   Because Italy is an ally of Nazi Germany, Italian Canadians are designated "enemy aliens."

1941   Joe DiMaggio, playing for the New York Yankees, hits safely in 56 consecutive baseball games, a record unparalleled in the history of the game.

1941-
1945   World War II: More than 500,000 Italian Americans serve in the United States armed forces.

1945-
1967   Italians emigrate to Canada during the post-war period and make up 70 percent of the Italian-Canadian population.

1946   Mother Cabrini is canonized a saint.

1946   John Pastore is elected governor of Rhode Island; he is the first Italian American elected governor of a state.

1950   Pastore is elected senator from Rhode Island, the first Italian American elected to the United States Senate.

1952   Rocky Marciano wins the heavyweight championship title, which he successfully defends six times.

1962   Anthony Celebrezze is appointed by President John F. Kennedy to serve as Secretary of Health, Education, and Welfare; he is the first Italian American to serve in United States Cabinet.

1965   The Immigration Reform Act passed in the United States, loosening restrictions on immigration for people of all nationalities.

1967   Columbus Day is declared a national holiday in the United States.

1967   Italian immigration to Canada drops significantly as a result of restrictive laws.

1968   Mario Bernardi is appointed first conductor of Ottawa's National Arts Center Orchestra and leads it to international fame.

1971   The Italian Canadian Benevolent Corporation is founded in Toronto to offer social services to Italians in Canada.

1974   The National Congress of Italian Canadians is founded in Ottawa to bring unity to Italian organizations in Canada.

1977   Governor Michael Dukakis of Massachusetts admits that the state erred in its prosecution and execution of Sacco and Vanzetti.

1981   Charles Caccia is appointed the first Italian federal cabinet minister in Canada.

1984   Geraldine Ferraro is nominated for vice president of the United States by the Democratic Party.

GLOSSARY

Alps: A range of mountains along the northern border of Italy.

Apennines: A range of mountains running down the center of Italy, forming the "backbone" of the peninsula.

Canonization: The final step in the process by which a person is declared a saint by the Roman Catholic Church.

Cente tabernacoli: Italian for "small shrine"; used in religious processions that are part of a *festa.*

Chain migration: the process by which an extended family of immigrants would arrive in North America, with initial arrivals making it possible for later immigrants to follow them.

Contadini: Small farmers; sometimes translated as "peasants."

Fascists: An Italian political party, marked by anti-democratic goals and methods, which was in power from 1922 through 1945.

Festa: Italian for "feast"; a religious ceremony often accompanied by elaborate celebrations and processions.

Libretto: The words to an opera.

"Little Italy": A generic name given to communities or neighborhoods in North American cities where large numbers of Italian immigrants lived.

Mafia: A reputed crime organization, supposedly controlled by Italians.

Marshall Plan: The massive assistance to western Europe from the United States after World War II which allowed countries such as Italy to rebuild their shattered economies.

Mezzogiorno: The Italian name for the south of Italy.

Mozzarella: A mild Italian cheese.

Mutual aid society: Organizations formed by Italian immigrants to assist one another with health care, insurance needs, and social contacts.

Padrone: Any Italian labor boss who contracted with employers to bring workers from Italy to North America.

Paese: A city, region, or area in Italy; in North America, the term was applied to neighborhoods where many Italians lived.

Paesani: Countrymen, compatriots; inhabitants of the same *paese.*

Parmesan: A hard Italian cheese with a slightly nutty flavor.

Pasta: A noodle made out of a combination of flour, eggs, and water, mixed to form a dough and cut into shapes that are allowed to dry and are then stored for future used. Varieties include *vermicelli*, thin noodles; *fettuccine*, broad, flat noodles; *manicotti*, tubes that are stuffed with meats or cheeses; and *conchiglie*, or noodles shaped like shells.

Prosciutto: An Italian variety of ham, often served in thin slices.

Renaissance: Literally meaning "rebirth," this term refers to the period following the Middle Ages in Europe when culture, learning, and artistic expression flourished. Generally considered to have begun in Italy in the fourteenth century.

Ricotta: A soft Italian cheese similar to cottage cheese but smoother.

Risorgimento: Italian for "resurrection"; the name given to the popular movement during the nineteenth century to unify the Italian peninsula's city-states into single nation.

Romance language: A language, such as Italian, that is derived from the Latin spoken in areas once ruled by the Roman Empire.

Romano: A hard Italian cheese, similar to but sharper than parmesan.

SMSA: Standard metropolitan statistical area, a designation used by the United States Bureau of the Census in determining population centers.

Truck farming: The planting, cultivation, and harvesting of fruit and vegetable produce for sale in markets, especially in cities.

Vendetta: A feud between families, often lasting for generations.

RESOURCES

America-Italy Society
38 E. 57th Street, New York, NY 10022
Founded: 1949. Members: 1,400.

The society promotes appreciation of the cultural heritage and contributions of Italy, especially in North America. It sponsors cultural exchanges, tours, workshops, and Italian-language classes for adults in New York City.

American-Italian Congress
111 Columbia Heights
Brooklyn, NY 11201
Founded: 1949

A federation of organizations which supports greater appreciation of the contributions made by Italian Americans to American political, social, cultural, and economic life. The federation grants awards to college students, sponsors essay contests, and maintains a research library with much biographical information. It also maintains the Italian Hall of Fame and the Brooklyn Hall of Fame.

Americans of Italian Descent
51 Madison Avenue, Suite 2902, New York, NY 10010
Founded: 1965. Members: 30,000

A civil rights organization dedicated to fighting defamation and discrimination against Americans of Italian descent. The organization is active in monitoring legislation, distributing publications, and supporting popular entertainment.

Italian-American Chamber of Commerce
126 W. Grand Avenue, Chicago, IL 60610
Founded: 1907. Members: 300

Promotes trade between the United States and Italy by offering information services, data banks, and other material to businesses and companies in both countries. Publishes a newsletter.

Italian-American Cultural Society
2811 Imperial Avenue, Warren, MI 48093
Founded: 1957. Members: 2,500.

Encourages appreciation of the contributions Italy and Italians have made to the United States and Canada. Offers placement services, sponsors competitions and awards to stress the importance of Italian cultural achievements, publishes a newsletter, and hosts an annual conference.

Italy-America Chamber of Commerce
350 Fifth Avenue, New York, NY 10118
Founded: 1887. Members: 750.

Actively sponsors greater economic ties between Italy and the United States. The Chamber provides a library with statistical and information services to business, industry, and commerce. Presents the Golden Globe Award (not to be confused with the film prize) to those who contribute to advances in international trade. Publishes an annual directory, a biweekly newsletter, and a bimonthly magazine, *Trade with Italy*.

National Italian-American Foundation
666 11th St, NW, Suite 800, Washington, DC 20001
Founded: 1975.

A government liaison and lobbying organization, designed to advance the interests of Italian Americans. Provides information services and a speakers' bureau, grants scholarships to individuals doing studies in areas of interest to Italian Americans, and publishes a monthly newsletter.

BIBLIOGRAPHY

Alba, Richard D. *Italian Americans: Into the Twilight of Ethnicity*. Englewood Cliffs, N.J.: Prentice-Hall, 1985. A relatively short but detailed study of the history of Italian immigrants in the United States, and how their conditions and perspectives have changed over the years.

Allen, James Paul, and Eugene James Turner. *We the People: An Atlas of America's Ethnic Diversity*. New York: Macmillan, 1988. A thorough and comprehensive study of where immigrant populations have settled in the United States, with many excellent maps and short but highly informative essays on each nationality.

Amfitheatrof, Erik. *The Children of Columbus*. Boston: Little, Brown, 1973. A wide-ranging and generally informal discussion of the Italian experience in the United States, with particular emphasis on the role of prominent individual Italians.

Gallo, Patrick J. *Old Bread, New Wine: A Portrait of the Italian-Americans*. Chicago: Nelson-Hall, 1981. A largely personal look at this group of immigrants and how coming to the United States affected them and their descendants.

Gambino, Richard. *Blood of My Blood: The Dilemma of the Italian-Americans*. Garden City, N.Y.: Doubleday, 1974. A personal and often moving account of what it means to be both Italian and American.

Green, Rose Basile. *The Italian-American Novel*. Rutherford, N.J.: Fairleigh Dickinson University Press, 1974. An extremely thorough study of almost every significant Italian-American novelist since the earliest days of America literature. An essential starting place for any study of the contributions made by Italian Americans to literature.

Iorizzo, Luciano, and Salvatore Mondello. *The Italian Americans*. Rev. ed. Boston: Twayne, 1980. A thorough examination of Italian immigrants to the United States, reviewing their history, culture, and social, religious, and political lives. The work uses many specific examples to make its points.

LoGatto, Rev. Anthony. *The Italians in America, 1492-1972*. Dobbs Ferry, N.Y.: Oceana Publications, 1972. Basically a chronology and data book, this volume contains much important information in a brief format.

Lourdeaux, Lee. *Italian and Irish Filmmakers in America*. Philadelphia: Temple University Press, 1990. A critical study of how these two cultures have influenced American movies, especially through the careers of notable directors such as Frank Capra and Francis Ford Coppola.

Nelli, Humbert S. *From Immigrants to Ethnics: The Italian Americans*. Oxford, England: Oxford University Press, 1983. A brief but thorough discussion of the Italian experience in the United States, viewed from a historical perspective. Provides a good overview of the influence of America and on its Italian immigrants and of the immigrants' effect on America.

Rolle, Andrew F. *The Immigrant Upraised: Italian Adventurers and Colonists in an Expanding America*. Norman: University of Oklahoma Press, 1968. A thorough examination of a contribution of Italian immigrants: their role in settling the frontier. Well researched and documented.

Scarpaci, Vincenza. *A Portrait of the Italians in America*. New York: Charles Scribner's Sons, 1982. A comprehensive yet intimate overview of the various conditions Italians have found in the United States, and their adaptations to them.

Zucchi, John E. *Italians in Toronto: Development of a National Identity, 1875-1935*. Kingston and Montreal: McGill-Queen's University Press, 1988. A specialized but informative book on the Italian experience in Canada. The study covers the period when most Italian immigrants entered Canada.

MEDIA BIBLIOGRAPHY

TELEVISION

Baretta (1975-1978). The title character, Detective Tony Baretta, was the orphaned son of Italian immigrants. A tough, unconventional cop, Baretta is a master of disguise and a quick-witted, wisecracking enforcer of law and order.

Columbo (1971-1977). With his rumpled raincoat and disheveled appearance, Lieutenant Columbo of the Los Angeles Police Department seems a well-meaning but bumbling character. Actually, he is a sharp-witted and observant detective, able to solve the toughest cases.

Delvecchio (1976-1977). Dominick Delvecchio is a Los Angeles police detective who solves cases ranging from narcotics violations to murder. His father, Tomaso, is a typical Old World Italian immigrant who has a small barbershop.

The Eddie Capra Mysteries (1978-1979). The hero of this series is a detective with a difference: He works for a law firm and not the police.

The Fanelli Boys (1990-   ). The story of a "typical" urban Italian-American family, whose three brothers share an apartment with their widowed mother. A broad comedy that often relies on ethnic stereotypes for its humor.

The Frank Sinatra Show (1950-1952; 1957-1958). These two series were an attempt to translate Sinatra's popularity in films to television; they had only limited success. The shows emphasized variety and singing acts, as well as some comedy.

Happy Days (1974-1984). Arthur "Fonzie" Fonzarelli is the Italian-American character in this popular comedy, set in 1950's middle-class America. On the surface, Fonzie is a tough, leather-jacketed biker, but underneath he has a warm heart and a sympathetic nature.

Hill Street Blues (1981-1987). This highly regarded crime drama revolves around Captain Frank Furillo, a complex and three-dimensional police officer who runs the often chaotic Hill Street Station while battling the problems in his own life, including alcoholism and a broken marriage.

The Jimmy Durante Show (1954-1957). This program, a showcase of

93

musical and variety talent, was hosted by Jimmy Durante. Set in the Club Durante, the show presented talent acts with Jimmy as emcee.

Johnny Staccato (1959-1960). Johnny Staccato was a jazz musician who earned extra money as a private eye. When not playing piano at Waldo's jazz club in Greenwich Village, Staccato was out on the mean streets, solving crimes.

The Perry Como Show (1945-1963). Easy-listening musical numbers, relaxed banter between the host and his guest stars and a warm, affectionate atmosphere made this show popular for many years.

Petrocelli (1974-1976). Tony Petrocelli, a Harvard-educated lawyer, moved west to practice in a small town, where he ended up solving crimes that baffled the local police.

The Untouchables (1959-1963). Set in the violent world of 1930's Chicago, this series featured an ongoing struggle between Special Agent Eliot Ness and his incorruptible team, and Al Capone and the Mob. Early episodes were protested because of the negative image they projected of Italians.

NOVELS

Arleo, Joseph. *The Grand Street Collector*, 1970. Based on an actual political assassination of an exiled Italian political leader in New York City, this novel traces the influences that politics, personal honor, and the immigrant experience have had on Italians in the United States. Fully realized characters and an economical style distinguish the novel.

Didonato, Pietro. *Christ in Concrete*, 1939. A poetic, autobiographical novel that explores the world of Italian immigrants, especially their exploitation and hardships. Paulie, the central character, is both an individual and a representative of all Italian immigrants.

Gallico, Paul. *The Small Miracle*, 1952. A deceptively simple, but actually very symbolic, story about Pepino, a young Italian boy who asks Saint Francis and the Pope to help cure his ill donkey, Violetta.

Paci, Frank. *Black Madonna*, 1982. Using the religious and cultural aspects of Italian-Canadian culture, Paci considers the various forces that shape people, both young and old, as they continue to develop.

————————. *The Father*, 1984. While concerned with the immigrant experience in Canada, this novel is more centered on the various individuals who are its characters. Paci's dual themes are, first, what it means to be an Italian Canadian and, second, what it means to be a specific person, regardless of background or nationality.

_____. *The Italians*, 1978. A realistic novel whose concern is the adjustments that Italian immigrants were forced to make in assimilating in Canadian society and, in turn, the effects which the Italians had on their new homeland.

Pei, Mario. *The Sparrows of Paris*, 1958. An exciting, carefully plotted novel that combines a detective story with a tale of the supernatural. Ancient occult rituals are linked with modern narcotics traffickers and political terrorists.

Puzo, Mario. *The Dark Arena*, 1955. Set in occupied Germany after World War II, this novel uses Walter Mosca, its central character, as a symbol of the dual nature of the modern human being: drawn to war while desiring peace, seeking justice while engaging in criminal activities.

_____. *The Fortunate Pilgrim*, 1964. Lucia Santa Angeluzzi-Corbo, an Italian immigrant to New York during the 1930's, is the central character of the novel. While she is a complete and recognizable individual herself, she is also a representative of the entire range of immigrant experience.

_____. *The Godfather*, 1969. The story of Don Vito Corleone and his dual families: his natural, or blood, family, and the Mafia family of which he is the head, or Godfather. More than a crime story, this is a meditation on the varieties of the immigrant experience in the United States.

FILMS

Buona Sera, Mrs. Campbell, 1969. In this lighthearted but socially conscious comedy, Carla, a young girl in a war-ravaged Italy, turns to three U.S. GI's for assistance. Years later, they return to Italy to see the daughter each of them believes he has fathered, and various complications follow.

The Godfather, 1972. The saga of the Corleone family, headed by Don Vito Corleone, the Godfather. Directed by Francis Ford Coppola, this sweeping film is more than a crime story; it is a view of one aspect of the Italian immigrant's experience in America.

The Godfather, Part II, 1974. The sequel to *The Godfather*, this film continues the story with Michael Corleone, the Godfather's son, who has followed in his father's footsteps. Contains scenes showing Don Vito Corleone's early days in America and how he came to be the Godfather.

The Godfather, Part III, 1990. With this film, Coppola completes the trilogy, showing how the Corleones found themselves changed, even destroyed, by the pressures of their violent lives and illegal business.

How to Murder Your Wife, 1965. After a wild party, a wealthy young bachelor cartoonist finds himself married to a young Italian girl who speaks no English. His daydreams about murdering her, expressed in his cartoons, lead to his trial. Finally, all is resolved.

Little Caesar, 1930. A bleak, uncompromising biography of an Italian criminal, Caesar Enrico Bandello, played by Edward G. Robinson. The scenes of Italian neighborhoods and the poverty endured by many early immigrants are powerful. Bandello is clearly based on Chicago's Al Capone, the mob leader.

Little Italy, 1921. A view of life in the Italian communities of New York. Sentimental in many spots, with characters who often come close to being stereotypes. Still, an early attempt to deal with this aspect of North American society in film.

Love Story, 1970. Jenny Cavilleri is the young, poor Italian girl who falls in love with a rich, spoiled Oliver Barrett IV. Their stormy but passionate relationship is followed in this romantic drama. She dies.

Marty, 1955. Marty Pilletti, played by Ernest Borgnine, is a lonely Italian butcher in Brooklyn. This film follows his search for companionship and happiness. A small-scale but often touching film about ordinary people and their lives.

Mean Streets, 1973. An episodic film that traces the days and nights of four young Italian Americans in their community in New York. Often violent, the film is filled with gritty, realistic detail.

Mister Antonio, 1929. A light, romantic film about typical Italians in the big city.

Rocky, 1976. Rocky Balboa is a young, not-too-bright lad who aspires to be a prizefighter. After many trials, he gets a shot at a title. A stirring account of a struggle against great odds.

The Rose Tattoo, 1955. Based on the play by Tennessee Williams, this is a smoldering story of passion and tangled love. Serafina Della Rose is played by the noted Italian actress Anna Magnani. Burt Lancaster is Alvaro Mangiacavallo.

Serpico, 1973. Based on the true story of Frank Serpico, the New York policeman who uncovered widespread corruption and payoffs in the city's police department. His revelations led to sweeping reforms in law enforcement.

Somebody Up There Likes Me, 1956. A fictionalized account of the life and career of Rocky Graziano, who came up from a tough Italian neighborhood to become middleweight boxing champion of the world. Paul Newman plays Rocky.

Splendor in the Grass, 1961. A tale of frustrated sexual desire among American teenagers, directed by Elia Kazan. Bud Stamper (played by Warren Beatty) finds true happiness when he marries Angelina, a poor Italian waitress, and makes a life for the couple on a small farm.

EDUCATIONAL FILMS

Ave Maria: The Story of the Fisherman's Feast, 1986. The center of this documentary is Boston's annual Festa del Madonna del Soccorso, or the "Fisherman's Feast," which is conducted in the New World much as it was in the Old. The annual feast, of Sicilian origin, combines elements of secular, religious, and pre-Christian traditions.

Dreams of Distant Shores, 1987. This is the story of European immigrants to the United States and Canada during the period 1890 through 1915, the time when most Italians crossed the Atlantic.

Hello, Columbus!, 1988. A documentary of the events leading up to and taking place during the annual Columbus Day celebrations in San Francisco. An excellent sampling of Italian customs, translated to North America.

Journey to Freedom, 1986. The story of the nineteenth century immigrants who settled in the eastern part of the United States, the region where most Italian Americans first established themselves.

The New Pilgrims, 1987. The effect that the immigrant has had on North American society, including the traditions and institutions of the United States, is sometimes overlooked. This study examines that influence, providing a different perspective on the issue.

When You Make a Good Crop: Italians in the Delta, 1988. A study of the traditions of Italian Americans in the Delta region of the Mississippi River. Shows how the experiences of the Old and New Worlds differ, how they are the same, and how they have blended.

AMERICAN VOICES

ITALIAN AMERICANS

INDEX